MW01129490

COOKING IN COSTA RICA

AN EXPAT'S GUIDE
TO BUYING GROCERIES,
COOKING, AND EATING
IN COSTA RICA

Gloria Yeatman

Copyright © 2017 by Gloria Yeatman
All rights reserved.
ISBN: 978-1977812162

Recipes from Costa Rica bloggers and cooks
were used with permission of the individual.

Published by Gloria Marie Yeatman

DEDICATION

For Paul, thank you for your love, support, and encouragement.
Without you, I wouldn't be on this great adventure.

And for Mom, from whom I inherited my love of cooking.

TABLE OF CONTENTS

❦ ❧

ACKNOWLEDGEMENTS

Thanks to my wonderful husband, Paul Yeatman, for proofreading my manuscript and suggesting improvements, my English language editor and friend, Jeni Giles Evans for helping me to be a more precise and less redundant writer, and to Ana Laura Vega and Carolina Álvarez, my Spanish language editors who ensured the accuracy of my translations.

Special thanks go to Costa Rica bloggers and cooks, Jen Beck Seymour, Chef Alex Corral, Debbie Hogue, Pat Wegner, and John Michael Arthur who allowed me to feature some of their recipes.

Thank you also to Loray Greiner from Hacienda Sur and Juan Bernardo Gamboa of the Tropical Grazing Institute who helped me to make sense of what various cuts of meat are called in Costa Rica.

And to all of the butchers, farmers, food vendors, home cooks, chefs, and waiters whom I have encountered in Costa Rica, thank you for your patience with my limited Spanish and for helping me *con mucho gusto* (with much pleasure).

What's Inside & How to Use This Book

When you move to a Spanish-speaking country, it can be daunting to stock your kitchen and cook meals when you don't know what your ingredients are called in Spanish. And even when you *know* the Spanish translation, it can be a challenge at times to find what you are looking for. So make it fun and think of it as a scavenger hunt!

My hope is that English-speaking expats and immigrants will find this book a practical guide and on-going reference tool when shopping for groceries and cooking both familiar and new foods in Costa Rica. You can download the electronic version of this book on your smart phone or iPad so you have it with you whenever you shop.

The table of contents is set up so you can easily turn to the meat section when you are at the butcher shop (*carnicería*) or to the dairy section when you are standing in front of the dairy case. If you want to translate a specific food like apple (*manzana*), you can use the Alphabetical Food Dictionary and click on "A" for apple (English to Spanish) or "M" for *manzana* (Spanish to English). Or, you can use the Food Dictionary by Category and look under "Fruits" (English to Spanish) or "*Frutas*" (Spanish to English).

Here's what you will find inside:

- A little bit about me, our life in Costa Rica, how and where we shop for groceries, what we spend, and some insights about grocery shopping in Costa Rica.

- An English-to-Spanish and Spanish-to-English food dictionary, broken down into the following sections:
  - Fruits
  - Vegetables
  - Meat & Poultry
  - Fish & Seafood
  - Grains, Nuts, Seeds, & Baking Ingredients
  - Dairy & Eggs, Refrigerated & Frozen Foods
  - Beans, Canned & Prepared Foods
  - Herbs, Spices, & Seasonings
  - Condiments
  - Beverages
- An English-to-Spanish and Spanish-to-English food dictionary in alphabetical order.
- An English-to-Spanish and Spanish-to-English dictionary of things you find in the kitchen.
- A Glossary of cooking terms and helpful adjectives to use when buying and cooking food, ordering in a restaurant, and reading recipes in Spanish.
- Recipe substitutions for when you can't find familiar ingredients here in Costa Rica.
- Recipes which I have adapted to use with ingredients found in Costa Rica, plus some favorite recipes of other expat cooks in Costa Rica.
- A U.S. Measure to Metric Conversion Guide for temperature, volume, weight, and length.
- A resource section with links to expat cooking blogs, Facebook groups and pages, specialty products, and other food-related things.

Cooking, Eating, & Buying Food in Costa Rica

"For me, cooking is an expression of the land where you are and the culture of that place."
Wolfgang Puck

"I'm just someone who likes cooking and for whom sharing food is a form of expression."
Maya Angelou

Sometimes, it is the challenges of everyday life that can make or break your experience when living in a foreign country. We become so used to the way things are done back home, that stepping out of that bubble into the larger world can be intimidating. But, it can also be an adventure!

I've always loved to cook and bake (something I inherited from my Italian mother), so shopping for food and adapting my cooking methods and recipes was one of those big challenges for me. When we lived in the United States, our normal routine consisted of major grocery shopping on Sundays, stopping often after work to pick up fresh items for dinner, and a weekly adventure to Trader Joe's. We loved Trader Joe's—not only for the reasonably priced staples, nuts, and cheeses but also for the unique snacks and the new products they featured each week. In fact, it's one of the few things I miss about living in the States. But when we moved to Costa Rica in 2009, I had no idea where to find my favorite ingredients or if they even existed in this country.

Therefore, I started to read local recipe books and cooking magazines, most of which were written in Spanish. Trying to read recipes with a Spanish/English dictionary at hand is a great way to learn Spanish.

3

So is taking a cooking or baking class. About six months after we arrived, I signed up for a baking class offered by a local caterer. I knew it would be presented in Spanish, but I could understand the basics and figured I could translate the recipes afterwards. The hosts were kind enough to run their recipes through Google Translate, which helped some. However, a few phrases had me scratching my head. One that sticks out was the instruction to "snow the clear." Huh? Later, I realized that it meant to "beat the egg whites to peaks." That is when I first had the idea to write this book!

Over the years, I've learned the local names for more and more of the foods I buy. I've tried the local foods, adapted recipes, researched and found solutions to cooking challenges. I've even learned to use, if not remember, the metric system. This book is result of all my research, experimentation, successes (and failures!) and I hope it makes shopping and cooking in Costa Rica an easier and more satisfying experience for you.

Shopping for Groceries

In 2009, my husband, Paul, and I moved to San Ramón de Alajuela, Costa Rica. San Ramón is a good-sized coffee town in the country's western Central Valley. It is still a real Tico (Costa Rican) town, with its traditions and customs intact.

We estimate there are 200-300 *gringos* (North Americans or Europeans) who live in the greater San Ramón area for at least part of the year, so the ratio of Ticos to gringos is just what we were looking for. However, that lower concentration of gringos means that stores and restaurants are less likely to cater to our tastes.

There are several grocery stores in town, three of them owned by Walmart (Maxi Pali, Pali, and Mas x Menos). There are also a few locally owned stores, plus lots of convenience stores, called mini-supers, *pulperias,* or *abastecedores.*

The important thing to understand about grocery stores in Costa Rica is that there is no such thing as one-stop shopping. After living in Costa Rica for five years, we returned to Baltimore to sell our house. I remember going to the Giant grocery store where we used to shop every week. I just stood there in the front of the store, overwhelmed by all the choices! So many brands and varieties of everyday products and so many other choices of items I had never seen before. Wow! It was one-stop shopping at its best. I guess that after living in Costa Rica for years, I had become used to limited options. With fewer options, life becomes simpler and decisions become easier. The other side of the coin is that you cannot necessarily find everything you are looking for in one store, or sometimes, at all. Sometimes you have to hunt in multiple stores in multiple towns. As a result, I rarely comparison-shop any more. Instead, I tend to buy what I need when I see it because it may not be there later.

A case in point is when I found a recipe online for Thai Shrimp Soup that sounded delicious. It called for red curry paste, so I visited every store in San Ramón looking for it. I found yellow curry paste, but not red, in one store. I even checked in specialty stores I came across when we visited friends in other towns. I finally found red curry paste at Auto Mercado, a chain of higher-end grocery stores that carries a wider range of imported products. It is a good option for those hard-to-find items. At Auto Mercado, you can even find canned pumpkin and cranberry sauce in November for those U.S. expats who want to prepare a traditional Thanksgiving dinner. There are Auto Mercados located throughout the general San José area as well as in some of the larger beach towns. The closest one to us is in Alajuela, about an hour's drive from San Ramón, so it is a once-in-a-while trip for us, usually when we have other stops to make in the area.

Another option for buying products that aren't available in our town is PriceSmart. Like Auto Mercado, the closest PriceSmart to us is in Alajuela, about an hour away. PriceSmart is a membership club like Costco or Sam's Club. Membership costs $35 per year. While products bought there may *or may not* be less expensive than buying locally, they do offer many familiar product brands and hard-to-find items. Here are some of the groceries we buy at PriceSmart when we go every few months:

- blocks of feta, cheddar, Swiss, and Parmesan cheeses
- pure maple syrup
- large bags of walnuts, almonds, and pecans

- large bags of chocolate chips
- extra virgin coconut oil
- McCormick pure vanilla extract
- good quality California olive oil
- good quality Balsamic vinegar
- large bags of frozen blueberries

As time has gone on, and we have found more products locally, we head to PriceSmart less frequently; though the above products are what we tend to buy on a regular basis.

Costa Rica grows great fruits and vegetables that are plentiful and inexpensive. Since the local *feria* (farmers' market) is only open on weekends, we often buy fresh produce in one of the many stands and shops nearby. One of our favorites is *La Gran Bodega de las Frutas y Verduras*. In addition to the store in San Ramón, they currently have other locations in Alajuela and Grecia. One of the best things about buying at Gran Bodega is that all of their products are from Costa Rica and they buy directly from the farms. You won't find GMO papayas from Hawaii here, just locally grown ones. They do offer some imported items like Granny Smith apples and big globe grapes. We eat lots of salads and Gran Bodega offers a variety of lettuces like red leaf, romaine, *lechuga americano* (similar to iceberg lettuce), frisée, and Boston lettuce.

In the States, I usually bought bags of pre-washed lettuce and baby spinach from Trader Joe's. However, in Costa Rica, lettuce comes in heads with dirt from the farm still clinging to it (though we are also starting to see more hydroponic lettuces and tomatoes available). If you plan to come to Costa Rica and love fresh salads, spend $10 on a salad spinner and pack it in your luggage. I use ours every day. I have seen them occasionally in stores like Auto Mercado, but they are about double the price.

While there seem to be bakeries on every other corner in Costa Rica, it is rare to find the kind of artisan and whole grain breads we like. My solution has been to bake my own, everything from pita bread to cinnamon raisin bread, banana bread, and *focaccia*. Baking my own is also a lot less expensive and the variety is endless. Lately, I have even started experimenting with sourdough breads and crackers. It is a bit more time intensive, especially remembering to feed my sourdough starter (which I've named "Bubbles").

The way eggs are sold in Costa Rica is different from in the States. Back home, I could go to the grocery store and buy a dozen medium, large, or extra-large eggs in the dairy case. In Costa Rica, eggs are sold by weight, either in trays or in bags, so you will most likely find an assortment of sizes in the same lot. Another difference is that eggs are not sold refrigerated in Costa Rica, which may seem unsafe at first. There is a good reason though. In the U.S., the USDA requires that all eggs from U.S. farms be power-washed since many factory-farmed chickens carry salmonella. That washing removes the protective coating that is on eggs when they were laid. Because of this practice, eggs in the U.S. are refrigerated to prevent them from spoiling. In Costa Rica, as in many other countries, eggs are not washed before they go to market. They are just gently cleaned, so it is not unusual to find a feather or two sticking to an eggshell. Since the protective coating that nature has provided is left intact, and as long as the hen laying the egg is healthy, the eggs remain fresh and safe to eat. I have to admit, once I get the eggs home, I still tend to refrigerate them.

The Feria

Most towns of any size have a weekly farmers' market, called a *feria*, one of the best places to shop for groceries. We go to the *feria* every week to buy just-picked fruits and vegetables, meats, fresh flowers, and more. It is also a great place to socialize with both locals and other expats. Most of the produce comes from family farms in the greater San Ramón area as well as from Zarcero, a prime growing area about 45 minutes away and higher up in the mountains. Some vendors at the *feria* sell imported Granny Smith and Red Delicious apples, navel oranges, red and green grapes, and Haas avocados.

Most *ferias* take place during the weekend, though they may occur on other days of the week. Our *feria* in San Ramón runs from 6:30 am to 9 pm on Fridays and continues on Saturday mornings from 7 am until noon. The best time to go is on Friday afternoon when there is the largest variety of offerings and the vendors have posted the prices.

In addition to fruits and vegetables of every kind, we can buy fresh chicken and meats, fish (including prepared *ceviche*), eggs, local cheeses, homemade hot sauce and tomato paste. There are also Costa Rican tamales and traditional sweets, ice cream, flowering and decorative plants, and herbs (both in plant form and freshly harvested), as well as artisan granola and *tapa dulce* (evaporated cane juice, sold in blocks or ground, like brown sugar). We can buy a *pipa*, a locally grown green coconut, have the vendor slice the top off with his machete, and drink the *agua de pipa* (coconut water) straight from the coconut with a straw. We have a friend who buys about a dozen at a time and has the vendor drain the coconut water into a jar; she later uses the coconut water for her smoothies. (Friends who visit the feria in Escazú tell me that there is a *pipa* vendor who sells coconut water by the liter.) We can buy Himalayan salt in various grinds, organic coffee, high quality coconut oil, dark chocolate and even homemade ginger beer. There are also vendors at our *feria* selling clothing, handmade purses and backpacks, pots and pans, handmade jewelry, and other items. In some towns, folks are lucky enough to have artisan bakers selling their products at the *feria*.

Unfamiliar Fruits and Vegetables

When you visit a produce market or *feria* in Costa Rica, you will see many familiar fruits and vegetables - lettuce, carrots, cucumbers, onions, pineapples, papayas, and mangoes; they are all there. However, there are other fruits and vegetables that most of us foreigners have never seen.

There are strange looking fruits like purple *caimitos* that look like a star inside when you cut them, and rust colored *zapotes* that look like big, soft yams. You will see yellow *nance* fruit that are usually sold in their husks, looking a bit like small tomatillos. There are *granadillas* (a type of passion fruit), *guanabana* (soursop), *guayabas* (guavas), and *guabas*, which look like big green boomerangs. And there are always *pejibaye*, with their orange or yellow skins and black stripes, sold boiled at both *ferias* and grocery stores. And then there is one of my favorites, *mamón chino* (rambutan or lychee), with their red or yellow spiked outer peels and flesh that tastes a bit like green grapes.

8

There are also some unfamiliar vegetables available in Costa Rica. There are tubers and root vegetables like *ñampi* and *tiquisque* that are used in the Tico favorite *Olla de Carne; arracacha,* which looks a bit like a turnip; and of course the ubiquitous *yuca* (also spelled *yucca*), with its dark brown skin and creamy white interior. The *yuca* plant, which is a member of the agave family, also produces stems of white flowers that you see for sale along the sides of the road and at the *feria* around Easter time. The flowers are known as *flor de itabo* in Costa Rica and the blossoms are traditionally scrambled with eggs and onions or in a hash called *picadillo*. You may find *chaya*, also known as *chicasquil*, which is a kind of tree spinach and can be prepared the same way as the spinach we know. One vegetable that was unfamiliar to me which we now eat regularly is *chayote*. Chayote is a member of the squash family, and it is common to see the vines growing in Tico gardens or climbing their fences. Chayote comes in various colors: dark green, light green, and a cream color, though I find the light green variety easier to peel. You will often see it served in restaurants cooked in a milk-based sauce along with corn and chopped carrots. I sometimes peel, slice, and steam it, serving the chayote with olive oil and seasonings, or use it in soups and stews.

And then, there are the familiar items you probably *won't* find. Yellow lemons, for instance, are almost unheard of in Costa Rica, though they may be found in some areas of the country on a limited basis. When you ask for *limón* (lemon) in Costa Rica, you will usually be offered either green limes or *mandarinos*. *Mandarinos* are green on the outside and bright orange and juicy on the inside. They may look like an orange when you cut them, but they are definitely sour like a lemon or lime. Of course, I had to try biting into one just to be sure! *Mandarinos* are my favorites. I use their juice wherever lemon or lime juice is called for in a recipe, in vinaigrettes, key lime pie, lemonade, etc. The taste is a little different from other types but we really like it.

Organic Produce

The demand for organic produce increases every year. It is easier to find organic produce in Costa Rica these days, even in chain stores like Walmart, though the selection is limited. Upward Spirals has put together an Organic Directory, a collection of more than 60 locations around the country to buy organic produce in Costa Rica. The Organic Directory is available for free download in both English and Spanish. Check the Resource section at the end of this book for download information.

In our town of San Ramón, we buy most of our organic produce at *Frutas y Verduras La Paquereña*. Every Friday morning, they receive deliveries from two organic farms located in Zarcero, Costa Rica: *Finca Organica Guadelupe*, a certified organic farm, and *Finca Organica Tierra de Sueños*, which, though no longer certified organic, still maintains their organic practices and values. Since the farms only deliver organic produce to *La Paquereña* once each week, the best time for us to shop is on Friday mornings to ensure the best selection.

Once you have found a source of organic produce near where you live, ask when they receive their deliveries from the farms to ensure you are getting not only the freshest produce but will have the best selection from which to choose.

There are also organic delivery services that allow you to order produce and other products online. You place your order by a certain time each week and then you pick up your order in a central location in your town or they deliver it to your home.

A great place to buy organic produce, for those folks living the Central Valley, is the *Feria Verde* farmers market in Aranjuez, San Jose. It is open on Saturday mornings from 7 am to 12:30 pm. Here you can find a variety of fresh, organic vegetables, fruits, legumes, tubers, and grains, plus meats, chicken, eggs and fish raised in sustainable ways. You can also buy prepared foods made with organic ingredients, such as preserves, jams, ice cream, bakery, sweets, dressings, wines, and coffee. The *Feria Verde* is also a great place for community, where you can enjoy tasty foods and browse the stands selling jewelry, clothing, ceramics, shoes, home care and personal care products.

Meats

A *carnicería* (butcher shop) in Costa Rica may seem full of "mystery meat" to our North American eyes. Not only are the names of everything in Spanish, but the cuts of meat are different from what we find in U.S. supermarkets. A pork chop may look the same in Costa Rica, but try finding chicken drumsticks, or a T-bone steak. While you can find some familiar cuts by knowing the Spanish translation, for some items, there are simply no equivalent cuts in Costa Rica. You may be able to find some familiar cuts in specialty meat markets or at PriceSmart; however, your local butcher shop may have no idea what you are looking for. At the *feria* in our town, there is a vendor who sells delicious ham. We buy it occasionally for sandwiches, or have them cut a ham steak for us. Where there is ham, I thought, there would be ham bones that I could use to make a pot of ham and bean soup. However, when I talked to the vendor, he had no idea what a *hueso de jamon* (ham bone) was. Recently though, at PriceSmart, I finally saw packaged bone-in hams like the ones available in the States.

Researching the Costa Rican names of cuts of meat was a bit of a challenge as well. It did not work to translate the North American name into literal Spanish. In fact, the same cut of meat may be called one thing in Costa Rica, something different in Mexico, and something totally different in another Spanish-speaking country. Also, the same cut of meat may be called by various names in different *carnicerías* and grocery stores. Therefore, where there is more than one common name for a cut of meat, I have listed each in the food dictionary.

Even in restaurants, there are differences between what we expect familiar-sounding dishes to be and what the waiter brings us. For instance, when you see *fajitas* on a menu, you may be expecting the typical Mexican presentation, with tortillas, sour cream, grilled peppers and onions, salsa, and cheese. However, in Costa Rica, fajitas are usually strips of beef or chicken, maybe with a bit of peppers and onions if you are lucky, and served without the usual accompaniments.

Health Food Stores

Health food stores in Costa Rica are called *macrobioticas,* and every town usually has a couple, at least. Some are better than others, offering a broad array of supplements, vitamins, and natural products, along with knowledgeable staff. Other stores are extremely limited in both their stock and expertise.

You never know what you will find in a *macrobiotica*. Years ago, when I was looking for molasses, I found it at a *macrobiotica,* not in a grocery store. Some *macrobioticas* sell fresh aloe vera leaves, natural soaps and toothpastes, and even whole grain breads. As with other types of shopping in Costa Rica, there is rarely one-stop shopping at a *macrobiotica.* The products offered are limited, often expensive, and rarely consistently available.

What We Eat and Spend for Groceries

One of the great things about living in Costa Rica is the year-round growing season. Coming from Baltimore, Maryland, we were limited to flavorless tomatoes throughout the winter months and often chose to go without. Now, we have fresh tomatoes, lettuce, pineapples, mangoes, and so much more, available to us all the time. Costa Rica is a fruit and vegetable lover's heaven! There are peak times when certain items are more plentiful and less expensive, just as there are low times when some items either disappear from the stores or are more expensive. For instance, though they are available year-round, mangoes are the most plentiful and least expensive in April and May. In March, the bright yellow casaba melons are in season and we have driven past farm stands where you can buy five for 1,000 colones (about $2).

We love fresh salads and fruits and vegetables of all kinds. Most of the produce we buy is locally grown, though some items, like Granny Smith apples, pears, and grapes, are imported. My husband, Paul, starts every day with a fruit smoothie. We buy fresh pineapple and papaya at the *feria,* which I cube and freeze, along with strawberries, for his smoothies. I even make fresh coconut milk from the flesh of the *pipas* we buy. And we start every day with a tall glass of water with fresh-squeezed *limón.*

We eat most of our meals at home. I love to cook and homemade food is usually so much healthier than what we can get eating out. Cooking at home also means I can control the quality and quantity of the ingredients. Generally, we do not eat meat with breakfast or lunch, unless it's leftovers from the night before. Dinner is the meat meal, usually with 3-6 ounces of meat, though we do have vegetarian meals a few times each week. We accompany our evening meal with a big salad or mounds of vegetables. I cook a variety of soups and stews and serve them with homemade bread or crackers. We also eat whole-grain rice (*arroz integral*), black beans, and, occasionally, pasta.

We are not regular drinkers of alcoholic beverages, though I enjoy an occasional glass of wine, so that holds our costs down. By making these choices, and limiting expensive imported items, we are able to keep our grocery budget to about $350 per month, on average. If you would like to read more about how much *we* spend to live here, check out *Our 2016 Annual Cost of Living in Costa Rica Summary*. (See the "Resources" section at the end of this book for the webpage.)

Remember, what *you* would spend on groceries in Costa Rica depends on many factors, such as the amount of imported products you buy, the amount of prepared vs. homemade foods you consume, how often you eat out in restaurants, whether alcoholic beverages are part of your regular shopping budget, and even where you live. If you live in a tourist or beach town, you will probably pay more for everything from milk to meals out.

Spanish Usage Guide

As a general rule, all Spanish words and phrases throughout this book are shown in *italics*. Spanish translations in the food dictionary and glossary are shown in ***bold italics***.

Now for a word about nouns, verbs, and adjectives included in the following sections. In Spanish, all nouns are either masculine or feminine, and as such, the article preceding them and any adjectives must agree in both number and gender.

Nouns and Their Articles

The feminine articles for the word "the" are *la* (singular) and *las* (plural) and for "a" or "an" the indefinite article is *una*. The masculine articles for "the" are *el* (singular) and *los* (plural) and for "a" or "an" the indefinite article is *un*.

Examples:
la remolacha - the beet
las uvas - the grapes
una cerveza - a beer
el maiz - the corn
los tomates - the tomatoes
un aguacate - an avocado

For the purpose of this shopping guide, and to keep things simple, articles are not included when translating English to Spanish. You should know, however, that they are used in conversation and may be included in recipes.

Adjectives

Adjectives must agree in both gender and number with the noun; and adjectives ending in "o" (masculine) change to "a" when used with a feminine noun.

Examples:
repollo crudo - raw cabbage
repollos crudos - raw cabbages
zanahoria cruda - raw carrot
zanahorias crudas - raw carrots

Throughout this guide, adjectives ending in "o" or "a" that change depending on the masculine and feminine nouns will be shown in this manner:

Examples:
crudo/a - raw
pequeño/a - small
unos/as - some

Verbs

Instructional verbs in recipes tend to use either the infinitive form (ending in -ar, -er, or -ir), or the third person singular (usted) of the imperative tense. Therefore, verbs included in this guide will show both forms, first the infinitive, followed by the imperative. Verb phrases are listed in either tense. This should help you recognize the verbs commonly used in recipes written in Spanish.

Examples:
medir, mida - to measure
cocinar, cocine - to cook
dorar, dore - to brown
dore por ambos lados - brown on both sides

Food Dictionary by Category - English to *Spanish*

❧ Fruit - *Frutas* ❧

apple - *manzana*
apricot - *albaricoque*
apricots, dried - *albaricoques secos*
avocado - *aguacate*
banana - *banano*
blackberries - *moras*
blueberries - *arándanos azules*
cantaloupe - *melón*
cape gooseberry - *uchuva*
casaba melon - *melón de casaba*
cashew fruit - *marañon*
cherry - *cereza*
coconut - *coco*
coconut water - *agua de pipa*
coconut, green - *pipa*
cranberries - *arándanos, arándanos rojos*
custard apple - *anona*
figs - *higos*
fruit - *fruta*
grapefruit - *toronja*
grapes - *uvas*
grapes, green - *uvas verdes*
grapes, purple - *uvas moradas*
grapes, seedless - *uvas sin semillas*

guava - *guayaba*
Jamaican plum - *jocote*
Japanese plum - *níspero*
kiwi - *kiwi*
lime - *limón*
lychee - *mamón chino*
mandarin lime - *limón mandarino*
mango - *mango*
nectarine - *nectarina*
orange - *naranja*
papaya - *papaya*
passion fruit - *maracuyá, granadilla*
peach - *melocotón*
peach palm - *pejibaye*
pear - *pera*
pineapple - *piña*
plantain - *plátano*
plantain, green - *plátano verde*
plum - *ciruela*
prunes - *ciruelas pasas*
rambutan - *mamón chino*
raspberries - *frambuesas*
shoemaker fruit - *nance, nanzi*
sour guava - *cas*
soursop - *guanábana*
star apple - *caimito*
star fruit - *carambola*
strawberries - *fresas*
tangerine - *mandarina*
water apple - *manzana de agua*
watermelon - *sandía*

৵ Vegetables - *Vegetales* ৵

artichoke - *alcachofa*
artichoke hearts - *corazones de alcachofa*
arugula - *rúcula, arúgula*
asparagus - *espárragos*
asparagus spears - *lanzas de espárragos*
avocado - *aguacate*
bean sprouts - *frijoles nacidos*
beet - *remolacha*
bell pepper - *chile morrón*
Bok Choy - *bok choy, pak choi*
broccoli - *brócoli*
Brussels sprouts - *coles de Bruselas*
button mushroom - *champiñon pequeño*
cabbage, Chinese - *mostaza china*
cabbage, green - *repollo verde*
cabbage, purple - *repollo morado*
carrot - *zanahoria*
cauliflower - *coliflor*
celery - *apio*
cherry tomatoes - *tomates cherry*
Chinese snow peas - *vainicas chinas*
corn - *maíz*
corn on the cob - *elote*
corn, sweet - *maíz dulce*
cucumber - *pepino*
eggplant - *berenjena*
endive - *escarola*
fennel - *hinojo*
frisée - *frisee*
garlic - *ajo*
green beans - *vainicas*
hearts of palm - *palmitos*
hot chili pepper - *chile picante*

jalapeño - *chile jalapeño*
kale - *kale*
leek - *puerro*
lettuce - *lechuga*
lettuce, iceburg - *lechuga americana*
lettuce, romaine - *lechuga romana*
lima beans - *frijoles de lima*
mushrooms - *hongos*
onion - *cebolla*
parsnip - *chirivía*
peas - *guisantes verdes, petit pois, arvejas verdes*
potato - *papa*
pumpkin - *calabaza*
purple onion - *cebolla morada*
radicchio - *achicoria*
radish - *rábano, rabano rojo*
scallions - *cebollinos*
shallots - *echalotes*
spinach - *espinaca*
sprouts - *brotes*
squash (winter or hard) - *ayote*
string beans - *vainicas*
sweet pepper - *chile dulce*
sweet potato - *camote*
sweet potato, orange - *camote naranja, camote zanahoria*
swiss chard - *acelga*
tomato - *tomate*
turnip - *nabo*
vegetable pear - *chayote*
vegetables - *vegetales, legumbres, verduras*
yuca - *yucca, yuca*
zucchini - *zucchinni, zapallito, calabazin, zukini*

❧ Meat & Poultry - *Carnes y Aves de Corral* ❧

back leg of... - *pierna de...*
bologna - *mortadela*
blood sausage - *morcilla de cerdo*
bones - *huesos*
brains - *sesos*
breakfast sausage - *salchicha desayuno*
cheeks - *cachetes*
chunks of... - *trocitos de...*
crown roast of... - *corona de...*
cutlet, thinly cut meat or poultry - *milanesa*
gizzards - *mollejas*
heart - *corazon*
hot dog - *perro caliente, salchicha, salchicha frankfurter*
kidney - *riñon*
lamb - *cordero*
lard - *manteca, lardo*
liver - *hígado*
loin - *lomo*
meat - *carne*
meatballs - *albóndigas*
Mexican syle sausage - *chorizo*
oxtail - *cola de buey, rabo de buey*
paleta - *shoulder*
paté - *pate*
processed packaged meat - *embutidos*
rabbit - *conejo*
salami - *salami*
sausage - *salchichón, salchicha*
shredded meat - *carne mechada*
soup bones - *huesos para sopa*
tail - *rabo, cola*
tenderloin - *lomito*
tendon - *tendon*

tongue - *lengua*
tripe - *mondongo*

Poultry - *Aves de Corral*
chicken - *pollo*
chicken breasts - *pechugas de pollo*
chicken breasts on the bone with ribs - *pechuga entera*
chicken breasts, boneless & skinless - *pechuga filete*
chicken cutlets (or pounded breasts) - *milanesa de pollo*
chicken drummettes - *muslos de alas*
chicken drumsticks - *muslito de muslo*
chicken leg quarters - *muslos de pollo enteros*
chicken livers - *hígados de pollo*
chicken organs, necks & feet (mixed) - *menudo de pollo*
chicken thighs - *muslos de pollo*
chicken wings - *alas de pollo, alitas de pollo*
chicken, ground - *carne molida de pollo*
chicken, whole - *pollo entero limpio*
duck - *pato*
eggs - *huevos*
gizzards - *mollejas*
hen - *gallina*
poultry - *aves de corral*
rooster - *gallo*
turkey - *pavo*
turkey breast, frozen - *pechuga de pavo congelada*
turkey ham - *jamón de pavo*
turkey ham, smoked - *jamón de pavo ahumado*
turkey sausage - *salchicha de pavo*
turkey, whole, raw - *pavo entero crudo*
turkey, whole, roasted - *pavo entero asado al horno*

Beef - *Res*
beef steak - *bistec de res*
beef, cubes or pieces - *cubitos de res, trocitos de res*

beef, cutlets - *milanesa de res*
beef, fillet - *filete de res*
beef, ground - *carne molida de res*
beef, ground, prime - *carne molida de res especial*
beef, ground, regular - *carne molida de res corriente*
beef, kidneys - *riñones de res*
beef, liver - *hígado de res*
beef, shredded - *carne mechada de res*
cheeseburger - *hamburguesa con queso*
corned beef - *pecho curado de res*
hamburger - *hamburguesa*
pastrami - *pastrame de res*

Beef Forequarter Cuts - *Cuarto Delantero de Res*
beef, back ribs - *costilla de res*
beef, brisket - *pecho de res*
beef, chuck roll - *lomo de aguja de res*
beef, cowboy steak - *Delmonico con hueso*
beef, flank steak - *alipego de res, filete de flanco*
beef, foreshank, bone-in - *ratón delantero de res con hueso*
beef, hanging tender - *lomito de entraña de res*
beef, hump - *morro de res*
beef, inside skirt steak - *arrachera de res*
beef, mock tender - *cacho de paleta de res*
beef, outside skirt steak - *cecina de res*
beef, ribeye (lip on) roll - *lomo Delmonico, lomo entero de res, rib eye de res*
beef, ribeye bone-in - *Delmonico con hueso*
beef, shank - *jarrete de res*
beef, shank, cross-cut - *osobuco, ossobuco de res*
beef, short ribs - *costilla de res*
beef, shoulder clod - *corazón de paleta de res, posta de paleta de res*
beef, top blade - *lomo de paleta de res*

Beef Hindquarter Cuts - *Cuarto Trasero de Res*

beef, bottom round - *Solomo de res*
beef, chuck shoulder - *paleta de res*
beef, eye of round - *mano de piedra de res*
beef, gooseneck - *Solomo, mano de piedra, posta de ratón trasero de res*
beef, heel of round - *posta de ratón trasero de res*
beef, hind shank, bone-in - *ratón trasero de res con hueso*
beef, hind shank, boneless - *ratón trasero de res sin hueso*
beef, knuckle (Sirloin tip) - *bolita de res*
beef, Porterhouse steak - *porter house de res*
beef, skirt steak - *falda de res*
beef, strip loin - *lomo ancho de res*
beef, tail - *rabo de res*
beef, T-bone steak - *t-bone de res*
beef, tenderloin - *lomito de res*
beef, tenderloin, bone-in - *lomito de res con hueso*
beef, top round, inside round, or rump - *posta de cuarto de res*
beef, top sirloin butt, center cut sirloin - *vuelta de lomo de res*
beef, top sirloin cap steak - *punta de solomo de res*
beef, tri-tip - *cacho de vuelta de lomo de res, gallinilla*

Veal - *Ternera*
osso buco (cross-cut veal shanks) - *ossobuco de res de ternera*
veal cutlet - *carne para milanesa de ternera*
veal roast - *posta de res de ternera*
veal, eye of round - *mano de piedra de res de ternera*
veal, leg of - *pierna de res de ternera*
veal, loin - *lomo de res de ternera*
veal, shank - *jarrete de ternera*
veal, short ribs - *costillas de res de ternera*
veal, sirloin - *sirloin de res de ternera*
veal, T bone - *T bone de res de ternera*
veal, tenderloin - *lomito de res de ternera*

Pork - *Cerdo*
bacon - *tocineta, tocino*

bacon, smoked - *tocineta ahumada*
ham - *jamón*
ham end - *punta de jamon*
ham steak - *filete de jamón*
ham, smoked - *jamón ahumado*
pigs feet - *manitas de cerdo, patas de cerdo*
pork - *cerdo, carne de cerdo*
pork, baby back spare ribs - *costilla de cerdo baby back*
pork, boneless tenderloin - *lomo de cerdo*
pork, chop - *chuleta de cerdo*
pork, chop, smoked - *chuleta de cerdo ahumada*
pork, cracklings - *chicharrones*
pork, cutlet - *milanesa de cerdo*
pork, flank steak - *falda de cerdo*
pork, ground - *carne molida de cerdo, molida de cerdo*
pork, lard - *manteca de cerdo, lardo de cerdo*
pork, leg - *pierna de cerdo*
pork, leg with skin - *pierna de cerdo con piel*
pork, roast - *posta de cerdo*
pork, shoulder roast - *posta de paleta de cerdo*
pork, spare ribs - *costillas de cerdo*
pork, tenderloin - *lomito de cerdo*
prosciutto - *jamón prosciutto*

Lamb - *Cordero*
lamb chops - *chuletas de cordero*
lamb shank - *jarrete de cordero*
lamb, breast - *asado de cordero*
lamb, leg of - *pierna de cordero*
lamb, ribs - *costillas de cordero*
lamb, shoulder chop - *espadilla de cordero*
sheep - *ovejas, carneros*

❧ Fish & Seafood - *Pescados y Mariscos* ❧

anchovy - *anchoa*
caviar - *caviar*
clam - *almeja*
cod - *bacalao*
crab - *cangrejo*
eel - *anguila, congrio*
fish - *pescado*
haddock - *abadejo*
herring - *arenque*
lobster - *langosta*
mackerel - *macarela, caballa, escombro*
mahi mahi - *dorado*
mussels - *mejillones*
octopus - *pulpo*
oyster - *ostra*
prawn - *gamba*
red snapper - *pargo rojo*
salmon - *salmón*
sardine - *sardina*
scallop - *vieira*
sea bass - *corvina*
seafood or shellfish - *mariscos*
shrimp - *camarón, camarónes*
squid - *calamares*
trout - *trucha*
tuna - *atún*
turbot - *rodaballo, rapante*

❧ Grains, Nuts, Seeds, & Baking Ingredients-*Granos, Nueces, Semillas, y Ingredientes Para Hornear* ❧

almonds - *almendras*

arborrio rice - *arroz para risotto, arroz "arborrio"*

artificial sweetener - *endulzante artificial, edulcorante artificial*

baking powder - *polvo para hornear*

baking soda - *bicarbonato, bicarbonato de sodio*

barley - *cebada*

bread - *pan*

bread, sliced - *pan rebanado*

bread, sourdough - *pan de masa madre*

bread crumbs - *pan rallado*

breadsticks - *grissini, palitos de pan*

brown rice - *arroz integral*

brown sugar - *azúcar moreno*

cake - *queque*

cane sugar, unrefined, ground - *tapa de dulce molida*

carrot cake - *queque de zanahoria*

cashews - *semillas de marañón*

cereals - *cereales*

cocoa - *cacao*

coconut, shredded - *coco rallado*

confectioners sugar - *azúcar blanco de plantación molido, azúcar glacé, azúcar en polvo*

cookies or crackers - *galletas*

corn - *maíz*

corn pancakes - *chorreadas*

corn starch - *fécula de maíz, maicena*

corn tortilla - *tortilla de maíz*

cous cous - *cús-cús*

cranberries, dried - *arándanos secos, arándanos deshidratados*

cream of tartar - *cremor tartaro*

croutons - *crutons*

dried fruits - *frutas secas*

enriched pasta - *pasta enriquecida*
filo pastry - *pasta filo*
flax seeds - *semillas de linaza*
flax seeds, ground - *linaza molida*
flour - *harina*
flour, all-purpose - *harina común*
flour, pastry or cake - *harina de repostería*
flour, wheat - *harina de trigo*
flour, whole grain - *harina integral*
glazing sugar - *azúcar glacé, azúcar blanco de plantación molido, azúcar en polvo*
hazelnut - *avellana*
hominy - *maíz cáscara*
honey - *miel, miel de abeja*
lady fingers - *dedos de señora*
lasagna - *lasaña*
lemon zest - *rayadura de limón*
macademia nuts - *macadamias*
macaroni - *macarrón*
mixed fruit peel - *corteza variada de fruta*
mixed nuts - *nueces mixtas, nueces mezcladas, nueces variadas*
molasses - *melaza*
noodles - *fideos*
nutmeg - *nuez moscada*
nuts - *nueces*
oatmeal - *avena*
oats, quick cooking - *avena mosh, avena "rapido" or "al minuto"*
oats, rolled - *hojuelas de avena integral*
oats, whole grain - *avena integral*
pasta, enriched - *pasta enriquecida*
pasta, fresh - *pasta fresca*
pasta, penne - *plumas, pasta penne*
peanuts - *maní*
pecans - *pecanas*
pine nuts - *piñones*

pistachio - *pistacho*
popcorn - *palomitas de maíz*
powdered sugar - *azúcar en polvo, azúcar glacé, azúcar blanco de plantación molido*
prunes - *ciruelas pasas*
puff pastry - *pasta de hojaldre*
raisins - *pasas*
rice - *arroz*
rice, arborio - *arroz arborio, arroz para risotto*
rice, brown/whole grain - *arroz integral*
rice, long grain - *arroz de grano largo*
rice, short grain - *arroz de grano corto*
salt - *sal*
seeds - *semillas*
semolina - *sémola*
sesame seeds - *semillas ajonjoli*
soda crackers - *galletas soda*
spaghetti - *espagueti*
sugar - *azúcar*
sugar substitute - *sustituto de azúcar*
sunflower seeds - *semillas girasol*
tortilla - *tortilla*
tortilla chips - *tortillas horneadas de maíz*
tortillas, corn - *tortillas de maíz*
tortillas, wheat - *tortillas de trigo*
vanilla extract - *vainilla, esencia de vainilla*
vanilla bean - *vaina de vainilla*
walnuts - *nuez, nueces*
wheat - *trigo*
wheat flour - *harina de trigo*
wheat tortilla - *tortilla de harina*
whole grain flour - *harina integral*
yeast - *levadura*

❧ Dairy & Eggs, Refrigerated & Frozen Foods - *Lácteos y Huevos, Refrigerados y Congelados* ❧

asiago cheese - *queso asiago*

blue cheese - *queso azul*

brie - *queso brie frances*

butter - *mantequilla*

butter, low-fat - *mantequilla baja en grasa*

butter, stick of - *barra de mantequilla*

buttermilk - *leche agria* (literally "sour milk")

Camembert - *queso camembert frances*

caramel sauce, milk-based - *dulce de leche*

Chantilly cream - *crema chantillí*

cheddar cheese - *queso cheddar*

cheese - *queso*

cheese, mild, semisoft - *queso semiduro*

cheese, shredded - *queso desmenuzado*

cottage cheese - *queso "cottage"*

cow's milk - *leche de vaca*

cream cheese - *queso crema, queso Philadelphia*

dairy products - *productos lácteos*

egg white - *clara de huevo*

egg yolk - *yema de huevo*

eggs - *huevos*

evaporated milk - *leche evaporada*

feta cheese - *queso feta*

fresh soft cheese - *queso fresco tierno*

frozen food - *alimentos congelados*

goat cheese - *queso de cabra*

goat's milk - *leche de cabra*

gouda - *queso gouda*

ice - *hielo*

ice cream - *helado*

margarine - *margarina*

milk - *leche*

milk, condensed - *leche condensada*
milk, evaporated - *leche evaporada*
milk, lactose-free - *leche deslactosada*
milk, powdered - *leche en polvo*
milk, reduced-fat (2%) - *leche semi-descremada 2% grasa*
milk, skimmed - *leche descremada*
mozzarella - *queso mozarela*
mozzarella, baby - *queso bocconcini*
orange juice - *jugo de naranja*
orange juice, freshly squeezed - *jugo de naranja ricién exprimido*
parmesan cheese - *queso parmesano*
Pecorino romano - *queso pecorino*
pudding, instant - *pudin instantaneo*
ricotta - *queso ricotta*
sheep's milk - *leche de oveja*
sheep's milk cheese - *queso de oveja*
sour cream - *natilla*
soy cheese - *queso de soya*
sweetened condensed milk - *dulce leche*
sweetened whipped cream - *crema chantillí*
whipped cream - *nata montada, crema batida*
whipping cream - *crema dulce*
yogurt - *yogur*
yogurt, plain - *yogur natural*

◆ Beans, Canned & Prepared Foods - *Frijoles, Alimentos Enlatados y Preparados* ◆

almond milk - *leche de almendras*
bean sprouts - *frijoles nacidos*
beans, black - *frijoles negros*
beans, red - *frijoles rojos*
beans, refried - *frijoles molidos*
beans, soy - *frijoles de soya*
beans, white or navy - *frijoles blancos*
beans, whole - *frijoles enteros*
beef broth - *caldo de res*
candy - *confites, dulces*
canned goods - *productos enlatados*
chick peas - *garbanzos*
chicken broth - *caldo de pollo*
coconut cream (sweetened) - *crema de coco*
coconut milk - *leche de coco*
cookies - *galletas*
corn, canned, sweet - *maíz dulce entero enlatados*
crackers - *galletas*
cranberry sauce, jellied, canned - *jalea de arándanos*
dessert - *postre*
hominy - *maíz cáscara*
lady fingers - *dedos de señora*
lentils - *lentejas*
peaches, canned - *melocotones en conserva*
pickle slices - *pepinillo en rodajas*
pickles - *pepinillos*
potato chips - *papas tostadas*
snack food - *cosas de picar*
soup, canned - *sopa enlatada*
soy milk - *leche de soya*
soy products - *productos de soya*
split peas - *arvejas secas*

texturized soy protein - *soya texturizada*
tomato paste - *pasta de tomate*
tomato sauce - *salsa de tomate; salsa de pomodoro*
tomatoes, canned and diced - *tomates en trocitos*
vegetable broth - *caldo de vegetales*

❧ Herbs, Spices, & Seasonings - *Hierbas, Especias, y Sazonadores* ❧

annatto seed, ground - *achiote*
basil - *albahaca*
bay leaf - *hoja de laurel*
cardamon - *cardamomo*
celery seeds - *semillas de apio*
chives - *chyves*
cilantro, coriander - *culantro*
cinnamon - *canela*
cinnamon stick - *ramita de canela*
cloves - *clavos de olor*
cream of tartar - *cremor tartaro*
culantro - *culantro coyote*
cumin - *comino*
curry - *curry*
dill - *eneldo*
fennel - *hinojo*
fennel seeds - *semillas de hinojo*
garlic - *ajo*
garlic clove - *diente de ajo*
ginger root - *raíz de jengibre*
ginger, ground - *jengibre en polvo*
herbs - *hierbas*
herbs de provence - *hierbas provenzales*
Italian flat leaf parsley - *perejil plano*
Italian seasoning - *sazonador de hierbas italianas*
lemon basil - *albahaca de limón*
lemongrass - *zacate de limón*
marjoram - *mejorana*
mint - *menta*
mustard, dry, ground - *mostaza en polvo*
nutmeg - *nuez moscada*
nutmeg, dry, grated - *nuez moscada en polvo*

oregano - *orégano*
paprika - *paprika*
parsley - *perejil*
pepper, black - *pimienta negra*
pepper, cayenne - *pimienta cayena*
pepper, white - *pimienta blanca*
peppermint - *hierbabuena*
peppermint leaves - *hojitas de hierbabuena*
purple basil - *albahaca morada*
rosemary - *romero*
saffron - *azafrán*
sage - *salvia*
salt - *sal*
salt, smoked - *sal ahumada*
sea salt - *sal del mar, sal marina*
sea salt, Himalayan - *sal del mar Himalaya, sal marina Himalaya*
seasoning - *condimento*
star anis - *anís de estrella*
thyme - *tomillo*
turmeric - *cúrcuma*

❧ Condiments - *Condimentos* ❧

balsamic vinegar - *vinagre balsámico*
capers - *alcaparras*
chipotle chiles in adobo sauce - *chiles chipotle en salsa de adobo*
coconut cream (sweetened) - *crema de coco*
coconut milk - *leche de coco*
cooking spray - *spray de cocina, aceite en spray, aceite para rociar*
Dijon mustard - *mostaza Dijon*
dressing - *aderezo*
gelatin - *gelatina*
gelatin, unflavored - *gelatina sin sabor*
honey - *miel de abeja*
jam - *mermelada*
jelly - *jalea*
ketchup - *salsa de tomate, catchup, kétchup*
lard - *manteca, lardo*
lemon juice - *jugo de limón*
Lizano sauce - *salsa Lizano (used in gallo pinto)*
maple syrup - *miel de maple, sirope de maple*
mayonnaise - *mayonesa*
molasses - *melaza*
mustard - *mostaza*
mustard, Dijon - *mostaza Dijon*
oil - *aceite*
oil, canola - *aceite de canola*
oil, corn - *aceite de maiz*
oil, extra virgen olive - *aceite de oliva extra virgen*
oil, olive - *aceite de oliva*
oil, palm - *aceite de palma*
oil, sesame - *aceite de ajonjolí, aceite de sésamo*
oil, soy - *aceite de soya*
oil, vegetable - *aceite de vegetal*
olives - *aceitunas, olivas*
pineapple marmalade or jam - *mermelada de piña*

salsa - *salsa*
sauce - *salsa*
soy lecithin - *lecitina de soya en polvo*
soy sauce - *salsa de soya*
syrup - *sirope*
tomato paste - *pasta de tomate*
tomato sauce - *salsa de tomate, salsa de pomodoro*
tomatoes, canned and diced - *tomates en trocitos*
vinegar, balsamic - *vinagre balsámico*
vinegar, red wine - *vinagre de vino tinto*
vinegar, rice - *vinagre de arroz*
vinegar, white wine - *vinagre de vino blanco*
Worsteshire sauce - *salsa inglesa*

❧ Beverages - *Bebidas* ❧

aperitif - *aperitivo*
apple juice - *jugo de manzana*
beer - *cerveza*
beer with lime juice - *cerveza michelada*
beer, dark - *cerveza negra*
beer, draught - *cerveza de barril, cerveza cruda*
beer, imported - *cerveza de importación*
beer, non-alcoholic - *cervaza sin alcohol*
brandy - *coñac*
champagne - *champaña, champán*
chocolate milkshake - *batido de chocolate*
cider - *sidra*
cocktail - *cóctel*
coffee - *café*
coffee beans - *granos de café*
coffee liqueur - *licor de café*
coffee with milk - *café con leche*
coffee, black - *café negro*
coffee, dark roast - *café tueste oscuro*
coffee, decaffeinated - *café descafeinado*
coffee, ground - *café molido*
coffee, instant - *café instantáneo*
coffee, made in traditional Tico drip style - *café chorreado*
Coke, cola - *coca*
Costa Rican sugar cane liquor - *guaro, Cacique*
creme de menthe - *licor de menta*
drink - *bebida*
drinking water - *agua potable*
fruit drink with milk base - *refresco con leche*
fruit drink with water base - *refresco con agua*
fruit juice - *jugo de fruta*
gin - *ginebra*
ginger ale - *ginger ale, gin*

grapefruit juice - *jugo de toronja*
hot chocolate - *chocolate caliente*
ice - *hielo*
juice - *jugo*
lager - *cerveza rubia*
lemonade - *limonada*
liquor - *licor*
milk, cold - *leche fría*
mineral water, sparkling - *agua mineral con gas*
mineral water, flat - *agua mineral sin gas*
non-alcoholic - *sin alcohol*
on the rocks - *en las rocas*
orange juice - *jugo de naranja*
orange liqueur - *licor de naranja*
quinine water - *quinada*
rum - *ron*
rum and coke - *ron con coca*
scotch - *whisky escocés*
sherry - *jerez*
smoothie - *batido, licuado*
soft drinks, soda - *gaseoso*
tea - *té*
tea, black - *té negro*
tea, chamomile - *té manzanilla*
tea, green - *té verde*
tea, herbal - *té de hierbas*
tea, hot - *té caliente*
tea, iced - *té frío*
tea, mint - *té menta*
tequila - *tequila*
tomato juice - *jugo de tomate*
tonic water - *tónica*
vermouth - *vermut*
vodka - *vodka*
water - *agua*

water, bottled - *agua embotellada, una botella de agua*
whisky - *wiski, whisky*
wine - *vino*
wine, Bordeaux - *vino de bordeos*
wine, Burgundy - *vino Borgoña*
wine, port - *oporto*
wine, red - *vino tinto*
wine, rosé - *vino rosado*
wine, sparkling - *vino espumoso*
wine, sweet - *vino dulce*
wine, white - *vino blanco*
with ice - *con hielo*

Food Dictionary by Category - *Spanish* to English

❧ *Frutas* - Fruit ❧

agua de pipa - coconut water
aguacate - avocado
albaricoque - apricot
albaricoques secos - apricots, dried
anona - custard apple
arándanos, arándanos rojos - cranberries
arándanos azules - blueberries
banano - banana
caimito - star apple
carambola - star fruit
cas - sour guava
cereza - cherry
ciruela - plum
ciruelas pasas - prunes
coco - coconut
frambuesas - raspberries
fresas - strawberries
fruta - fruit
granadilla - a type of passion fruit
guanábana - soursop
guayaba - guava
higos - figs
jocote - Jamaican plum
kiwi - kiwi

limón - lime
limón mandarino - mandarin lime
mamón chino - rambutan, lychee
mandarina - tangerine
mango - mango
manzana - apple
manzana de agua - water apple
maracuyá - passion fruit
marañon - cashew fruit
melocotón - peach
melón - cantaloupe
melón de casaba - casaba melon
moras - blackberries
nance, nanzi - shoemaker fruit
naranja - orange
nectarina - nectarine
níspero - Japanese plum
papaya - papaya
pejibaye - peach palm
pera - pear
piña - pineapple
pipa - coconut, green
plátano - plantain
plátano verde - plantain, green
sandía - watermelon
toronja - grapefruit
uchuva - cape gooseberry, golden berry
uvas - grapes
uvas moradas - grapes, purple
uvas sin semillas - grapes, seedless
uvas verdes - grapes, green

❧ *Vegetales* - Vegetables ❦

acelga - swiss chard
achicoria - radicchio
aguacate - avocado
ajo - garlic
alcachofa - artichoke
apio - celery
arúgula - arugula
ayote - squash (winter or hard)
berenjena - eggplant
bok choy - Bok Choy
brócoli - broccoli
brotes - sprouts
calabaza - pumpkin
calabazin - zucchini
camote - sweet potato
camote naranja, camote zanahoria - sweet potato, orange
cebolla - onion
cebolla morada - purple onion
cebollinos - scallions
champiñon pequeño - button mushroom
chayote - vegetable pear
chile dulce - sweet pepper
chile jalapeño - jalapeño
chile morrón - bell pepper
chile picante - hot chili pepper
chirivía - parsnip
coles de Bruselas - Brussels sprouts
coliflor - cauliflower
corazones de alcachofa - artichoke hearts
echalotes - shallots
elote - corn on the cob
escarola - endive
espárragos - asparagus

espinaca - spinach
frijoles de lima - lima beans
frijoles nacidos - bean sprouts
frisee - frisée
guisantes verdes, petit pois, arvejas verdes - peas
hinojo - fennel
hongos - mushrooms
kale - kale
lanzas de espárragos - asparagus spears
lechuga - lettuce
lechuga americana - lettuce, iceburg
lechuga romana - lettuce, romaine
legumbres - vegetables
maíz - corn
maíz dulce - corn, sweet
mostaza china - Chinese cabbage
nabo - turnip
pak choi - Bok Choy
palmitos - hearts of palm
papa - potato
pepino - cucumber
puerro - leek
rábano, rabano rojo - radish
remolacha - beet
repollo morado - cabbage, purple
repollo verde - cabbage, green
rúcula - arugula
tomate - tomato
tomates cherry - cherry tomatoes
vainicas - green beans (string beans)
vainicas chinas - Chinese snow peas
vegetales - vegetables
verduras - vegetables
yuca, yucca - yuca
zanahoria - carrot

zapallito - zucchini
zucchinni - zucchini
zukini - zucchini

⤶ *Carnes y Aves de Corral* - Meat & Poultry ⤷

albóndigas - meatballs
cachetes - cheeks
carne - meat
carne mechada - shredded meat
chorizo - Mexican syle sausage
cola de buey, rabo de buey - oxtail
conejo - rabbit
corazon - heart
cordero - lamb
corona de... - crown roast of...
embutidos - processed packaged meat
hígado - liver
huesos - bones
huesos para sopa - soup bones
lardo - lard
lengua - tongue
lomito - tenderloin
lomo - loin
manteca - lard
milanesa - cutlet, thinly cut meat or poultry
mollejas - gizzards
mondongo - tripe
morcilla de cerdo - blood sausage
mortadela - bologna
pate - paté
perro caliente - hot dog
pierna de cordero - leg of lamb
pierna de... - back leg of...
rabo, cola - tail
riñon - kidney
salchicha - sausage, hot dog
salchicha desayuno - breakfast sausage
salchicha frankfurter - hot dog

salchichón - sausage
salami - salami
sesos - brains
shoulder - paleta
tendon - tendon
trocitos de... - chunks of...

Aves de Corral - Poultry

alas de pollo, alitas de pollo - chicken wings
aves de corral - poultry
carne molida de pollo - chicken, ground
gallina - hen
gallo - rooster
hígados de pollo - chicken livers
huevos - eggs
jamón de pavo - turkey ham
jamón de pavo ahumado - turkey ham, smoked
menudo de pollo - chicken organs, necks & feet (mixed)
milanesa de pollo - chicken cutlets (or pounded breasts)
mollejas - gizzards
muslito de muslo - chicken drumsticks
muslos de alas - chicken drummettes
muslos de pollo - chicken thighs
muslos de pollo enteros - chicken leg quarters
pato - duck
pavo - turkey
pavo entero asado al horno - turkey, whole, roasted
pavo entero crudo - turkey, whole, raw
pechuga de pavo congelada - turkey breast, frozen
pechuga entera - chicken breasts on the bone with ribs
pechuga filete - chicken breasts, boneless & skinless
pechugas de pollo - chicken breasts
pollo - chicken
pollo entero limpio - chicken, whole
salchicha de pavo - turkey sausage

Res - Beef

bistec de res - beef steak
carne mechada de res - beef, shredded
carne molida de res - beef, ground
carne molida de res corriente - beef, ground, regular
carne molida de res especial - beef, ground, prime
cubitos de res, trocitos de res - beef, cubes or pieces
filete de res - beef, fillet
hamburguesa - hamburger
hamburguesa con queso - cheeseburger
higado de res - beef, liver
milanesa de res - beef, cutlets
pastrame de res - pastrami
pecho curado de res - corned beef
riñones de res - beef, kidneys

Cuarto Delantero de Res - Beef Forequarter Cuts

alipego de res - beef, flank steak
arrachera de res - beef, inside skirt steak
cacho de paleta de res - beef, mock tender
cecina de res - beef, outside skirt steak
corazón de paleta de res, posta de paleta de res - beef, shoulder clod
costillas de res - beef, back ribs or short ribs
Delmonico con hueso - beef, cowboy steak or ribeye, bone-in
filete de flanco - beef, flank steak
jarrete de res - beef, shank
lomito de entraña de res - beef, hanging tender
lomo de aguja de res - beef, chuck roll
lomo de paleta de res - beef, top blade
lomo Delmonico, lomo entero de res, rib eye de res - beef, ribeye (lip on) roll
morro de res - beef, hump
osobuco, ossobuco de res - beef, shank, cross-cut
pecho de res - beef, brisket

ratón delantero de res con hueso - beef, foreshank, bone-in

Cuarto Trasero de Res - Beef Hindquarter Cuts
bolita de res - beef, knuckle (Sirloin tip)
cacho de vuelta de lomo de res, gallinilla - beef, tri-tip
falda de res - beef, skirt steak
lomito de res - beef, tenderloin
lomito de res con hueso - beef, tenderloin, bone-in
lomo ancho de res - beef, strip loin
mano de piedra de res - beef, eye of round
paleta de res - beef, chuck shoulder
porter house de res - beef, Porterhouse steak
posta de cuarto de res - beef, top round, inside round, or rump
posta de ratón trasero de res - beef, heel of round
punta de solomo de res - beef, top sirloin cap steak
rabo de res - beef, tail
ratón trasero de res con hueso - beef, hind shank, bone-in
ratón trasero de res sin hueso - beef, hind shank, boneless
Solomo de res - beef, bottom round
Solomo, mano de piedra, posta de ratón trasero de res - beef, gooseneck
t-bone de res - beef, T-bone steak
vuelta de lomo de res - beef, top sirloin butt, center cut sirloin

Ternera - Veal
carne para milanesa de ternera - veal cutlet
costillas de res de ternera - veal, short ribs
jarrete de ternera - veal, shank
lomito de res de ternera - veal, tenderloin
lomo de res de ternera - veal, loin
mano de piedra de res de ternera - veal, eye of round
ossobuco de res de ternera - Osso buco (cross-cut veal shanks)
pierna de res de ternera - veal, leg of
posta de res de ternera - veal roast
sirloin de res de ternera - veal, sirloin
T bone de res de ternera - veal, T bone

Cerdo - Pork
carne molida de cerdo, molida de cerdo - pork, ground
cerdo, carne de cerdo - pork
chicharrones - pork, cracklings (fried pork belly or fried pork rinds)
chuleta de cerdo - pork, chop
chuleta de cerdo ahumada - pork, chop, smoked
costilla de cerdo baby back - pork, baby back spare ribs
costillas de cerdo - pork, spare ribs
falda de cerdo - pork, flank steak
filete de jamón - ham steak
jamón - ham
jamón ahumado - ham, smoked
jamón prosciutto - prosciutto
lardo de cerdo - pork, lard
lomito de cerdo - pork, tenderloin
lomo de cerdo - pork, boneless tenderloin
manitas de cerdo - pigs feet
manteca de cerdo - pork, lard
milanesa de cerdo - pork, cutlet
patas de cerdo - pigs feet
pierna de cerdo - pork, leg
pierna de cerdo con piel - pork, leg with skin
posta de cerdo - pork, roast
posta de paleta de cerdo - pork, shoulder roast
punta de jamon - ham end
tocineta ahumada - bacon, smoked
tocineta, tocino - bacon

Cordero - Lamb
asado de cordero - lamb, breast
chuletas de cordero - lamb chops
costillas de cordero - lamb, ribs
espadilla de cordero - lamb, shoulder chop
jarrete de cordero - lamb shank

ovejas, carneros - sheep
pierna de cordero - lamb, leg of

❧ *Pescados y Mariscos* - Fish & Seafood ❧

abadejo - haddock
almeja - clam
anchoa - anchovy
anguila - eel
arenque - herring
atún - tuna
bacalao - cod
caballa - mackerel
calamares - squid
camarón, camarónes - shrimp
cangrejo - crab
caviar - caviar
congrio - eel
corvina - sea bass
dorado - mahi mahi
escombro - mackerel
gamba - prawn
langosta - lobster
macarela - mackerel
mariscos - seafood or shellfish
mejillones - mussels
ostra - oyster
pargo rojo - red snapper
pescado - fish
pulpo - octopus
rapante - turbot
rodaballo - turbot
salmón - salmon
sardina - sardine
trucha - trout
vieira - scallop

❧ *Granos, Nueces, Semillas, y Ingredientes Para Hornear*-Grains, Nuts, Seeds, & Baking Ingredients ❧

almendras - almonds

arándanos secos - cranberries, dried

arándanos deshidratados - cranberries, dried

arroz - rice

arroz arborio, arroz para risotto - rice, arborio

arroz de grano corto - rice, short grain

arroz de grano largo - rice, long grain

arroz integral - rice, brown/whole grain

arroz para risotto, arroz "arborrio" - arborrio rice

avellana - hazelnut

avena - oatmeal

avena integral - oats, whole grain

avena mosh, avena "rapido" or avena "al minuto" - oats, quick cooking

azúcar - sugar

azúcar blanco de plantación molido - confectioners sugar, glazing sugar, powdered sugar

azúcar en polvo - powdered sugar, confectioners sugar, glazing sugar

azúcar glacé - glazing sugar, confectioners sugar, powdered sugar

azúcar moreno - brown sugar

bicarbonato, bicarbonato de sodio - baking soda

cacao - cocoa

cebada - barley

cereales - cereals

chorreadas - corn pancakes

ciruelas pasas - prunes

coco rallado - coconut, shredded

corteza variada de fruta - mixed fruit peel

cremor tartaro - cream of tartar

crutons - croutons

cús-cús - cous cous

dedos de señora - lady fingers

endulzante artificial, edulcorante artificial - artificial sweetener

espagueti - spaghetti
fécula de maíz, maicena - corn starch
fideos - noodles
frutas secas - dried fruits
galletas - cookies or crackers
galletas soda - soda crackers
grissini - breadsticks
harina - flour
harina común - flour, all-purpose
harina de repostería - flour, pastry or cake
harina de trigo - flour, wheat
harina integral - flour, whole grain
hojuelas de avena integral - oats, rolled
lasaña - lasagna
levadura - yeast
linaza molida - flax seeds, ground
macadamias - macademia nuts
macarrón - macaroni
maíz - corn
maíz cáscara - hominy
maní - peanuts
miel, miel de abeja - honey
melaza - molasses
nueces - nuts
nueces mixtas, nueces mezcladas, nueces variadas - mixed nuts
nuez moscada - nutmeg
nuez, nueces - walnuts
palitos de pan - breadsticks
palomitas de maíz - popcorn
pan - bread
pan de masa madre - bread, sourdough
pan rallado - bread crumbs
pan rebanado - sliced bread
pasas - raisins
pasta de hojaldre - puff pastry

pasta enriquecida - pasta, enriched
pasta filo - filo pastry
pasta fresca - pasta, fresh
pecanas - pecans
piñones - pine nuts
pistacho - pistachio
plumas, pasta penne - pasta, penne
polvo para hornear - baking powder
queque - cake
queque de zanahoria - carrot cake
rayadura de limón - lemon zest
sal - salt
semillas - seeds
semillas ajonjoli - sesame seeds
semillas de linaza - flax seeds
semillas de marañón - cashews
semillas girasol - sunflower seeds
sémola - semolina
sustituto de azúcar - sugar substitute
tapa de dulce molida - cane sugar, unrefined, ground
tortilla - tortilla
tortilla de harina - wheat tortilla
tortilla de maíz - corn tortilla
tortillas horneadas de maíz - tortilla chips
trigo - wheat
vaina de vainilla - vanilla bean
vainilla, esencia de vainilla - vanilla extract

❧ Lácteos y Huevos, Refrigerados y Congelados - Dairy & Eggs, Refrigerated & Frozen Foods ❦

alimentos congelados - frozen food
barra de mantequilla - butter, stick of
clara de huevo - egg white
crema batida - whipped cream
crema chantillí - Chantilly cream
crema chantillí - sweetened whipped cream
crema dulce - whipping cream
dulce de leche - caramel sauce, milk-based
dulce leche - sweetened condensed milk
helado - ice cream
hielo - ice
huevos - eggs
jugo de naranja - orange juice
jugo de naranja ricién exprimido - orange juice, freshly squeezed
leche - milk
leche agria - buttermilk (literally "sour milk")
leche condensada - milk, condensed
leche de cabra - goat's milk
leche de oveja - sheep's milk
leche de vaca - cow's milk
leche descremada - milk, skimmed
leche deslactosada - milk, lactose-free
leche en polvo - milk, powdered
leche evaporada - milk, evaporated
leche semi-descremada 2% grasa - milk, reduced-fat (2%)
mantequilla - butter
mantequilla baja en grasa - butter, low-fat
margarina - margarine
nata montada - whipped cream
natilla - sour cream
productos lácteos - dairy products
pudin instantaneo - pudding, instant

queso - cheese
queso "cottage" - cottage cheese
queso asiago - asiago cheese
queso azul - blue cheese
queso bocconcini - mozzarella, baby
queso brie frances - brie
queso camembert frances - Camembert
queso cheddar - cheddar cheese
queso crema, queso Philadelphia - cream cheese
queso de cabra - goat cheese
queso de oveja - sheep's milk cheese
queso de soya - soy cheese
queso desmenuzado - cheese, shredded
queso feta - feta cheese
queso fresco tierno - fresh soft cheese
queso gouda - gouda
queso mozarela - mozzarella
queso parmesano - parmesan cheese
queso pecorino - Pecorino romano
queso ricotta - ricotta
queso semiduro - cheese, mild, semisoft
yema de huevo - egg yolk
yogur - yogurt
yogur natural - yogurt, plain

❧ *Frijoles, Alimentos Enlatados y Preparados* - Beans, Canned & Prepared Foods ❦

arvejas secas - split peas
caldo de pollo - chicken broth
caldo de res - beef broth
caldo de vegetales - vegetable broth
confites - candy
cosas de picar - snack food
crema de coco - coconut cream (sweetened)
dedos de señora - lady fingers
dulces - candy, sweets
frijoles blancos - beans, white or navy
frijoles enteros - beans, whole
frijoles molidos - beans, refried
frijoles nacido - bean sprouts
frijoles negros - beans, black
frijoles rojos - beans, red
frijoles de soya - beans, soy
galletas - cookies or crackers
garbanzos - chick peas
jalea de arándanos - cranberry sauce, jellied, canned
leche de almendras - almond milk
leche de coco - coconut milk
leche de soya - soy milk
lentejas - lentils
maíz cáscara - hominy
maíz dulce entero enlatados - corn, canned, sweet
melocotones en conserva - peaches, canned
papas tostadas - potato chips
pasta de tomate - tomato paste
pepinillo en rodajas - pickle slices
pepinillos - pickles
postre - dessert
productos de soya - soy products

productos enlatados - canned goods
salsa de pomodoro - tomato sauce
salsa de tomate - tomato sauce
sopa enlatada - soup, canned
soya texturizada - texturized soy protein
tomates en trocitos - tomatoes, canned and diced

❧ *Hierbas, Especias, y Sazonadores* - Herbs, Spices, & Seasonings ❧

achiote - annatto seed, ground
ajo - garlic
albahaca - basil
albahaca de limón - lemon basil
albahaca morada - purple basil
anís de estrella - star anis
azafrán - saffron
canela - cinnamon
cardamomo - cardamon
chyves - chives
clavos de olor - cloves
comino - cumin
condimento - seasoning
cremor tartaro - cream of tartar
culantro - cilantro, coriander
culantro coyote - culantro
cúrcuma - turmeric
curry - curry
diente de ajo - garlic clove
eneldo - dill
hierbabuena - peppermint
hierbas - herbs
hierbas provenzales - herbs de provence
hinojo - fennel
hoja de laurel - bay leaf
hojitas de hierbabuena - peppermint leaves
jengibre en polvo - ginger, ground
mejorana - marjoram
menta - mint
mostaza en polvo - mustard, dry, ground
nuez moscada - nutmeg
nuez moscada en polvo - nutmeg, dry, grated

orégano - oregano
paprika - paprika
perejil - parsley
perejil plano - Italian flat leaf parsley
pimienta blanca - pepper, white
pimienta cayena - pepper, cayenne
pimienta negra - pepper, black
raíz de jengibre - ginger root
ramita de canela - cinnamon stick
romero - rosemary
sal - salt
sal ahumada - salt, smoked
sal del mar - sea salt
sal marina - sea salt
sal del mar Himalaya - Himalayan sea salt
sal marina Himalaya - Himalayan sea salt
salvia - sage
sazonador de hierbas italianas - Italian seasoning
semillas de apio - celery seeds
semillas de hinojo - fennel seeds
tomillo - thyme
zacate de limón - lemongrass

❧ *Condimentos* - Condiments ❧

aceite - oil

aceite de ajonjolí - oil, sesame

aceite de canola - oil, canola

aceite de maiz - oil, corn

aceite de oliva - oil, olive

aceite de oliva extra virgen - oil, extra virgen olive

aceite de palma - oil, palm

aceite de sésamo - oil, sesame

aceite de soya - oil, soy

aceite de vegetal - oil, vegetable

aceite en spray - cooking spray

aceite para rociar - cooking spray

aceitunas, olivas - olives

aderezo - dressing

alcaparras - capers

chiles chipotle en salsa de adobo - chipotle chiles in adobo sauce

crema de coco - coconut cream (sweetened)

gelatina - gelatin

gelatina sin sabor - gelatin, unflavored

jalea - jelly

jugo de limón - lemon juice

lardo - lard

leche de coco - coconut milk

lecitina de soya en polvo - soy lecithin

manteca - lard

mayonesa - mayonnaise

melaza - molasses

mermelada - jam

mermelada de piña - pineapple marmalade or jam

miel de abeja - honey

miel de maple - maple syrup

mostaza - mustard

mostaza Dijon - mustard, Dijon

pasta de tomate - tomato paste
salsa - sauce, salsa
salsa Lizano (used in gallo pinto) - Lizano sauce
salsa de pomodoro - tomato sauce
salsa de soya - soy sauce
salsa de tomate, catchup, kétchup - ketchup
salsa de tomate - tomato sauce
salsa inglesa - Worsteshire sauce
sirope - syrup
sirope de maple - maple syrup
spray de cocina - cooking spray
tomates en trocitos - tomatoes, canned and diced
vinagre balsámico - vinegar, balsamic
vinagre de arroz - vinegar, rice
vinagre de vino blanco - vinegar, white wine
vinagre de vino tinto - vinegar, red wine

❧ *Bebidas* - Beverages ❧

agua - water
agua embotellada, una botella de agua - water, bottled
agua mineral con gas - mineral water, sparkling
agua mineral sin gas - mineral water, flat
agua potable - drinking water
aperitivo - aperitif
batido - smoothie or milkshake
batido de chocolate - chocolate milkshake
bebida - drink
café - coffee
café tueste oscuro - coffee, dark roast
café chorreado - coffee, made in traditional Tico drip style
café con leche - coffee with milk
café descafeinado - coffee, decaffeinated
café instantáneo - coffee, instant
café molido - coffee, ground
café negro - coffee, black
cervaza sin alcohol - beer, non-alcoholic
cerveza - beer
cerveza de barril, cerveza cruda - beer, draught
cerveza de importación - beer, imported
cerveza michelada - beer with lime juice
cerveza negra - beer, dark
cerveza rubia - lager
champaña, champán - champagne
chocolate caliente - hot chocolate
coca - Coke, cola
cóctel - cocktail
con hielo - with ice
coñac - brandy
en las rocas - on the rocks
gaseoso - soft drinks, soda
ginebra - gin

ginger ale, gin - ginger ale
granos de café - coffee beans
guaro, Cacique - Costa Rican sugar cane liquor
hielo - ice
jerez - sherry
jugo - juice
jugo de fruta - fruit juice
jugo de manzana - apple juice
jugo de naranja - orange juice
jugo de tomate - tomato juice
jugo de toronja - grapefruit juice
leche fría - milk, cold
licor - liquor
licor de café - coffee liqueur
licor de menta - creme de menthe
licor de naranja - orange liqueur
licuado - smoothie
limonada - lemonade
oporto - wine, port
quinada - quinine water
refresco con agua - fruit drink with water base
refresco con leche - fruit drink with milk base
ron - rum
ron con coca - rum and coke
sidra - cider
sin alcohol - non-alcoholic
té - tea
té caliente - tea, hot
té de hierbas - tea, herbal
té frío - tea, iced
té manzanilla - tea, chamomile
té menta - tea, mint
té negro - tea, black
té verde - tea, green
tequila - tequila

tónica - tonic water
vermut - vermouth
vino - wine
vino blanco - wine, white
vino Borgoña - wine, Burgundy
vino de bordeos - wine, Bordeaux
vino dulce - wine, sweet
vino espumoso - wine, sparkling
vino rosado - wine, rosé
vino tinto - wine, red
vodka - vodka
whisky escocés - scotch
wiski, whisky - whisky

Food Dictionary Alphabetical - English to *Spanish*

‿ A ᕽ

almond milk - *leche de almendras*
almonds - *almendras*
anchovy - *anchoa*
annatto seed, ground - *achiote*
aperitif - *aperitivo*
apple - *manzana*
apple juice - *jugo de manzana*
apricot - *albaricoque*
apricots, dried - *albaricoques secos*
arborrio rice - *arroz para risotto, arroz "arborrio"*
artichoke - *alcachofa*
artichoke hearts - *corazones de alcachofa*
artificial sweetener - *endulzante artificial, edulcorante artificial*
arugula - *rúcula, arúgula*
asiago cheese - *queso asiago*
asparagus - *espárragos*
asparagus spears - *lanzas de espárragos*
avocado - *aguacate*

‿ B ᕽ

back leg of... - *pierna de...*
bacon - *tocineta, tocino*
bacon, smoked - *tocineta ahumada*

baking ingredients - *ingredientes para hornear*
baking powder - *polvo para hornear*
baking soda - *bicarbonato, bicarbonato de sodio*
bologna - *mortadela*
balsamic vinegar - *vinagre balsámico*
banana - *banano*
barley - *cebada*
basil - *albahaca*
bay leaf - *hoja de laurel*
bean sprouts - *frijoles nacido*
beans - *frijoles*
beans, black - *frijoles negros*
beans, green (string beans) - *vainicas*
beans, red - *frijoles rojos*
beans, refried - *frijoles molidos*
beans, soy - *frijoles de soya*
beans, white or navy - *frijoles blancos*
beans, whole - *frijoles enteros*
beef - *res*
beef broth - *caldo de res*
beef steak - *bistec de res*
beef, back ribs - *costilla de res*
beef, bottom round - *Solomo de res*
beef, brisket - *pecho de res*
beef, chuck roll - *lomo de aguja de res*
beef, chuck shoulder - *paleta de res*
beef, cowboy steak - *Delmonico con hueso*
beef, cubes or pieces - *cubitos de res, trocitos de res*
beef, cutlets - *milanesa de res*
beef, eye of round - *mano de piedra de res*
beef, fillet - *filete de res*
beef, flank steak - *alipego de res, filete de flanco*
beef, foreshank, bone-in - *ratón delantero de res con hueso*
beef, gooseneck - *Solomo, mano de piedra, posta de ratón trasero de res*
beef, ground - *carne molida de res*

beef, ground, prime - *carne molida de res especial*
beef, ground, regular - *carne molida de res corriente*
beef, hanging tender - *lomito de entraña de res*
beef, heel of round - *posta de ratón trasero de res*
beef, hind shank, bone-in - *ratón trasero de res con hueso*
beef, hind shank, boneless - *ratón trasero de res sin hueso*
beef, hump - *morro de res*
beef, inside skirt steak - *arrachera de res*
beef, kidneys - *riñones de res*
beef, knuckle (Sirloin tip) - *bolita de res*
beef, liver - *hígado de res*
beef, mock tender - *cacho de paleta de res*
beef, outside skirt steak - *cecina de res*
beef, Porterhouse steak - *porter house de res*
beef, ribeye (lip on) roll - *lomo Delmonico, lomo entero de res, rib eye de res*
beef, ribeye bone-in - *Delmonico con hueso*
beef, shank - *jarrete de res*
beef, shank, cross-cut - *osobuco, ossobuco de res*
beef, short ribs - *costilla de res*
beef, shoulder clod - *corazón de paleta de res, posta de paleta de res*
beef, shredded - *carne mechada de res*
beef, skirt steak - *falda de res*
beef, strip loin - *lomo ancho de res*
beef, tail - *rabo de res*
beef, T-bone steak - *t-bone de res*
beef, tenderloin - *lomito de res*
beef, tenderloin, bone-in - *lomito de res con hueso*
beef, top blade - *lomo de paleta de res*
beef, top round, inside round, or rump - *posta de cuarto de res*
beef, top sirloin butt, center cut sirloin - *vuelta de lomo de res*
beef, top sirloin cap steak - *punta de solomo de res*
beef, tri-tip - *cacho de vuelta de lomo de res, gallinilla*
beer - *cerveza*
beer with lime juice - *cerveza michelada*

beer, dark - *cerveza negra*
beer, draught - *cerveza de barril, cerveza cruda*
beer, imported - *cerveza de importación*
beer, non-alcoholic - *cervaza sin alcohol*
beet - *remolacha*
bell pepper - *chile morrón*
beverages - *bebidas*
blackberries - *moras*
blood sausage - *morcilla de cerdo*
blue cheese - *queso azul*
blueberries - *arándanos azules*
Bok Choy - *bok choy, pak choi*
bones - *huesos*
brains - *sesos*
brandy - *coñac*
bread - *pan*
bread, sliced - *pan rebanado*
bread, sourdough - *pan de masa madre*
bread crumbs - *pan rallado*
breadsticks - *grissini, palitos de pan*
breakfast sausage - *salchicha desayuno*
brie - *queso brie frances*
broccoli - *brócoli*
brown rice - *arroz integral*
brown sugar - *azúcar moreno*
Brussels sprouts - *coles de Bruselas*
butter - *mantequilla*
butter, low-fat - *mantequilla baja en grasa*
butter, stick of - *barra de mantequilla*
buttermilk - *leche agria* (literally "sour milk")
button mushroom - *champiñon pequeño*

❧ C ☙

cabbage, Chinese - *mostaza china*

cabbage, green - *repollo verde*
cabbage, purple - *repollo morado*
cake - *queque*
Camembert - *queso camembert frances*
candy - *confites, dulces*
cane sugar, unrefined, ground - *tapa de dulce molida*
canned foods - *alimentos enlatados*
canned goods - *productos enlatados*
cantaloupe - *melón*
cape gooseberry - *uchuva*
capers - *alcaparras*
caramel sauce, milk-based - *dulce de leche*
cardamon - *cardamomo*
carrot - *zanahoria*
carrot cake - *queque de zanahoria*
casaba melon - *melón de casaba*
cashew fruit - *marañon*
cashews - *semillas de marañón*
cauliflower - *coliflor*
caviar - *caviar*
celery - *apio*
celery seeds - *semillas de apio*
cereals - *cereales*
champagne - *champaña, champán*
Chantilly cream - *crema chantillí*
cheddar cheese - *queso cheddar*
cheeks - *cachetes*
cheese - *queso*
cheese, mild, semisoft - *queso semiduro*
cheese, shredded - *queso desmenuzado*
cheeseburger - *hamburguesa con queso*
cherry - *cereza*
cherry tomatoes - *tomates cherry*
chick peas - *garbanzos*
chicken - *pollo*

chicken breasts - *pechugas de pollo*
chicken breasts on the bone with ribs - *pechuga entera*
chicken breasts, boneless & skinless - *pechuga filete*
chicken broth - *caldo de pollo*
chicken cutlets (or pounded breasts) - *milanesa de pollo*
chicken drummettes - *muslos de alas*
chicken drumsticks - *muslito de muslo*
chicken leg quarters - *muslos de pollo enteros*
chicken livers - *hígados de pollo*
chicken organs, necks & feet (mixed) - *menudo de pollo*
chicken thighs - *muslos de pollo*
chicken wings - *alas de pollo, alitas de pollo*
chicken, ground - *carne molida de pollo*
chicken, whole - *pollo entero limpio*
Chinese snow peas - *vainicas chinas*
chipotle chiles in adobo sauce - *chiles chipotle en salsa de adobo*
chives - *chyves, cebollinos*
chocolate milkshake - *batido de chocolate*
chunks of... - *trocitos de...*
cider - *sidra*
cilantro, coriander - *culantro*
cinnamon - *canela*
cinnamon stick - *ramita de canela*
clam - *almeja*
cloves - *clavos de olor*
cocktail - *cóctel*
cocoa - *cacao*
coconut - *coco*
coconut cream (sweetened) - *crema de coco*
coconut milk - *leche de coco*
coconut water - *agua de pipa*
coconut, green - *pipa*
coconut, shredded - *coco rallado*
cod - *bacalao*
coffee - *café*

coffee beans - *granos de café*
coffee liqueur - *licor de café*
coffee with milk - *café con leche*
coffee, black - *café negro*
coffee, dark roast - *café tueste oscuro*
coffee, decaffeinated - *café descafeinado*
coffee, ground - *café molido*
coffee, instant - *café instantáneo*
coffee, made in traditional Tico drip style - *café chorreado*
Coke, cola - *coca*
condiments - *condimentos*
confectioners sugar - *azúcar blanco de plantación molido, azúcar glacé, azúcar en polvo*
cookies - *galletas*
cooking spray - *spray de cocina, aceite en spray, aceite para rociar*
corn - *maíz*
corn on the cob - *elote*
corn pancakes - *chorreadas*
corn starch - *fécula de maíz, maicena*
corn tortilla - *tortilla de maíz*
corn, canned, sweet - *maíz dulce entero enlatados*
corn, sweet - *maíz dulce*
corned beef - *pecho curado de res*
Costa Rican sugar cane liquor - *guaro, Cacique*
cottage cheese - *queso "cottage"*
cous cous - *cús-cús*
cow's milk - *leche de vaca*
crab - *cangrejo*
crackers - *galletas*
cranberries - *arándanos, arándanos rojos*
cranberries, dried - *arándanos secos, arándanos deshidratados*
cranberry sauce, jellied, canned - *jalea de arándanos*
cream cheese - *queso crema, queso Philadelphia*
cream of tartar - *cremor tartaro*
creme de menthe - *licor de menta*

croutons - *crutons*
crown roast of... - *corona de...*
cucumber - *pepino*
culantro - *culantro coyote*
cumin - *comino*
curry - *curry*
custard apple - *anona*
cutlet, thinly cut meat or poultry - *milanesa*

❧ D-E ❧

dairy - *lácteos*
dairy products - *productos lácteos*
dessert - *postre*
Dijon mustard - *mostaza Dijon*
dill - *eneldo*
dressing - *aderezo*
dried fruits - *frutas secas*
drink - *bebida*
drinking water - *agua potable*
duck - *pato*
eel - *anguila, congrio*
egg white - *clara de huevo*
egg yolk - *yema de huevo*
eggplant - *berenjena*
eggs - *huevos*
endive - *escarola*
enriched pasta - *pasta enriquecida*
evaporated milk - *leche evaporada*

❧ F-G ❧

fennel - *hinojo*
fennel seeds - *semillas de hinojo*
feta cheese - *queso feta*

figs - *higos*
filo pastry - *pasta filo*
fish - *pescado*
flax seeds - *semillas de linaza*
flax seeds, ground - *linaza molida*
flour - *harina*
flour, all-purpose - *harina común*
flour, pastry or cake - *harina de repostería*
flour, wheat - *harina de trigo*
flour, whole grain - *harina integral*
forequarter cuts - *cuarto delantero*
fresh soft cheese - *queso fresco tierno*
frisée - *frisee*
frozen foods - *alimentos congelados*
fruit drink with milk base - *refresco con leche*
fruit drink with water base - *refresco con agua*
fruit juice - *jugo de fruta*
fruit - *fruta*
fruits - *frutas*
garlic - *ajo*
garlic clove - *diente de ajo*
gelatin - *gelatina*
gelatin, unflavored - *gelatina sin sabor*
gin - *ginebra*
ginger ale - *ginger ale, gin*
ginger root - *raíz de jengibre*
ginger, ground - *jengibre en polvo*
gizzards - *mollejas*
glazing sugar - *azúcar glacé, azúcar blanco de plantación molido, azúcar
   en polvo*
goat cheese - *queso de cabra*
goat's milk - *leche de cabra*
gouda - *queso gouda*
grains - *granos*
grapefruit - *toronja*

grapefruit juice - *jugo de toronja*
grapes - *uvas*
grapes, green - *uvas verdes*
grapes, purple - *uvas moradas*
grapes, seedless - *uvas sin semillas*
green beans - *vainicas*
green tea - *té verde*
guava - *guayaba*

❧ H-J ❦

haddock - *abadejo*
ham - *jamón*
ham end - *punta de jamon*
ham steak - *filete de jamón*
ham, smoked - *jamón ahumado*
hamburger - *hamburguesa*
hazelnut - *avellana*
heart - *corazon*
hearts of palm - *palmitos*
hen - *gallina*
herbs - *hierbas*
herbs de provence - *hierbas provenzales*
herring - *arenque*
hindquarter cuts - *cuarto trasero*
hominy - *maíz cáscara*
honey - *miel de abeja*
hot chili pepper - *chile picante*
hot chocolate - *chocolate caliente*
hot dog - *perro caliente, salchicha, salchicha frankfurter*
ice - *hielo*
ice cream - *helado*
iced tea - *té frío*
Italian flat leaf parsley - *perejil plano*
Italian seasoning - *sazonador de hierbas italianas*

jalapeño - *chile jalapeño*
jam - *mermelada*
Jamaican plum - *jocote*
Japanese plum - *níspero*
jelly - *jalea*
juice - *jugo*

ᕔ K-L ᕢ

kale - *kale*
ketchup - *salsa de tomate, catchup, kétchup*
kidney - *riñon*
kiwi - *kiwi*
lady fingers - *dedos de señora*
lager - *cerveza rubia*
lamb - *cordero*
lamb chops - *chuletas de cordero*
lamb shank - *jarrete de cordero*
lamb, breast - *asado de cordero*
lamb, leg of - *pierna de cordero*
lamb, ribs - *costillas de cordero*
lamb, shoulder chop - *espadilla de cordero*
lard - *manteca, lardo*
lasagna - *lasaña*
leek - *puerro*
lemon basil - *albahaca de limón*
lemon juice - *jugo de limón*
lemon zest - *rayadura de limón*
lemonade - *limonada*
lemongrass - *zacate de limón*
lentils - *lentejas*
lettuce - *lechuga*
lettuce, iceburg - *lechuga americana*
lettuce, romaine - *lechuga romana*
lima beans - *frijoles de lima*

lime - *limón*
liquor - *licor*
liver - *hígado*
Lizano sauce - *salsa Lizano (used in gallo pinto)*
lobster - *langosta*
loin - *lomo*
lychee - *mamón chino*

❧ M ❧

macadamia nuts - *macadamias*
macaroni - *macarrón*
mackerel - *macarela, caballa, escombro*
mahi mahi - *dorado*
mandarin lime - *limón mandarino*
mango - *mango*
maple syrup - *miel de maple, sirope de maple*
margarine - *margarina*
marjoram - *mejorana*
mayonnaise - *mayonesa*
meat - *carne*
meatballs - *albóndigas*
meats - *carnes*
Mexican syle sausage - *chorizo*
milk - *leche*
milk, cold - *leche fría*
milk, condensed - *leche condensada*
milk, evaporated - *leche evaporada*
milk, lactose-free - *leche deslactosada*
milk, powdered - *leche en polvo*
milk, reduced-fat (2%) - *leche semi-descremada 2% grasa*
milk, skimmed - *leche descremada*
mineral water, sparkling - *agua mineral con gas*
mineral water, flat - *agua mineral sin gas*
mint - *menta*

mixed fruit peel - *corteza variada de fruta*
mixed nuts - *nueces mixtas, nueces mezcladas, nueces variadas*
molasses - *melaza*
mozzarella - *queso mozarela*
mozzarella, baby - *queso bocconcini*
mushrooms - *hongos*
mussels - *mejillones*
mustard - *mostaza*
mustard, Dijon - *mostaza Dijon*
mustard, dry, ground - *mostaza en polvo*

ࣷ N-O ࣸ

nectarine - *nectarina*
non-alcoholic - *sin alcohol*
noodles - *fideos*
nutmeg - *nuez moscada*
nutmeg, dry, grated - *nuez moscada en polvo*
nuts - *nueces*
oatmeal - *avena*
oats, quick cooking - *avena mosh, avena "rapido" or "al minuto"*
oats, rolled - *hojuelas de avena integral*
oats, whole grain - *avena integral*
octopus - *pulpo*
oil - *aceite*
oil, canola - *aceite de canola*
oil, corn - *aceite de maiz*
oil, extra virgen olive - *aceite de oliva extra virgen*
oil, olive - *aceite de oliva*
oil, palm - *aceite de palma*
oil, sesame - *aceite de ajonjolí, aceite de sésamo*
oil, soy - *aceite de soya*
oil, vegetable - *aceite de vegetal*
olives - *aceitunas, olivas*
on the rocks - *en las rocas*

onion - *cebolla*
orange - *naranja*
orange juice - *jugo de naranja*
orange juice, freshly squeezed - *jugo de naranja rición exprimido*
orange liqueur - *licor de naranja*
oregano - *orégano*
osso buco (cross-cut veal shanks) - *ossobuco de res de ternera*
oxtail - *cola de buey, rabo de buey*
oyster - *ostra*

❧ P ❦

paleta - *shoulder*
papaya - *papaya*
paprika - *paprika*
parmesan cheese - *queso parmesano*
parsley - *perejil*
parsnip - *chirivía*
passion fruit - *maracuyá, granadilla*
pasta, enriched - *pasta enriquecida*
pasta, fresh - *pasta fresca*
pasta, penne - *plumas, pasta penne*
pastrami - *pastrame de res*
paté - *pate*
peach - *melocotón*
peach palm - *pejibaye*
peaches, canned - *melocotones en conserva*
peanuts - *maní*
pear - *pera*
peas - *guisantes verdes, petit pois, arvejas verdes*
pecans - *pecanas*
Pecorino romano - *queso pecorino*
pepper, black - *pimienta negra*
pepper, cayenne - *pimienta cayena*
pepper, white - *pimienta blanca*

peppermint - *hierbabuena*
peppermint leaves - *hojitas de hierbabuena*
pickle slices - *pepinillo en rodajas*
pickles - *pepinillos*
pigs feet - *manitas de cerdo, patas de cerdo*
pine nuts - *piñones*
pineapple - *piña*
pineapple marmalade or jam - *mermelada de piña*
pistachio - *pistacho*
plantain - *plátano*
plantain, green - *plátano verde*
plum - *ciruela*
popcorn - *palomitas de maíz*
pork - *cerdo, carne de cerdo*
pork, baby back spare ribs - *costilla de cerdo baby back*
pork, boneless tenderloin - *lomo de cerdo*
pork, chop - *chuleta de cerdo*
pork, chop, smoked - *chuleta de cerdo ahumada*
pork, cracklings - *chicharrones*
pork, cutlet - *milanesa de cerdo*
pork, flank steak - *falda de cerdo*
pork, ground - *carne molida de cerdo, molida de cerdo*
pork, lard - *manteca de cerdo, lardo de cerdo*
pork, leg - *pierna de cerdo*
pork, leg with skin - *pierna de cerdo con piel*
pork, roast - *posta de cerdo*
pork, shoulder roast - *posta de paleta de cerdo*
pork, spare ribs - *costillas de cerdo*
pork, tenderloin - *lomito de cerdo*
potato - *papa*
potato chips - *papas tostadas*
poultry - *aves de corral*
powdered sugar - *azúcar en polvo, azúcar glacé, azúcar blanco de
    plantación molido*
prawn - *gamba*

prepared foods - *alimentos preparados*
processed packaged meat - *embutidos*
prosciutto - *jamón prosciutto*
prunes - *ciruelas pasas*
pudding, instant - *pudin instantaneo*
puff pastry - *pasta de hojaldre*
pumpkin - *calabaza*
purple basil - *albahaca morada*
purple onion - *cebolla morada*

❧ Q-R ❧

quinine water - *quinada*
rabbit - *conejo*
radicchio - *achicoria*
radish - *rábano, rabano rojo*
raisins - *pasas*
rambutan - *mamón chino*
raspberries - *frambuesas*
red snapper - *pargo rojo*
refrigerated foods - *refrigerados*
rice - *arroz*
rice, arborio - *arroz arborio, arroz para risotto*
rice, brown, whole grain - *arroz integral*
rice, long grain - *arroz de grano largo*
rice, short grain - *arroz de grano corto*
ricotta - *queso ricotta*
rooster - *gallo*
rosemary - *romero*
rum - *ron*
rum and coke - *ron con coca*

❧ S ❧

saffron - *azafrán*

sage - *salvia*

salami - *salami*

salmon - *salmón*

salsa - *salsa*

salt - *sal*

salt, smoked - *sal ahumada*

sardine - *sardina*

sauce - *salsa*

sausage - *salchichón, salchicha*

scallions - *cebollinos*

scallop - *vieira*

scotch - *whisky escocés*

sea bass - *corvina*

sea salt - *sal del mar, sal marina*

sea salt, Himalayan - *sal del mar Himalaya, sal marina Himalaya*

seafood - *mariscos*

seasonings - *sazonadores, condimentos*

seeds - *semillas*

semolina - *sémola*

sesame seeds - *semillas ajonjoli*

shallots - *echalotes*

sheep - *ovejas, carneros*

sheep's milk - *leche de oveja*

sheep's milk cheese - *queso de oveja*

sherry - *jerez*

shoemaker fruit - *nance, nanzi*

shredded meat - *carne mechada*

shrimp - *camarón, camarónes*

smoothie - *batido, licuado*

snack food - *cosas de picar*

soda crackers - *galletas soda*

soft drinks, soda - *gaseoso*

soup bones - *huesos para sopa*

soup, canned - *sopa enlatada*

sour cream - *natilla*

sour guava - *cas*
soursop - *guanábana*
soy cheese - *queso de soya*
soy lecithin - *lecitina de soya en polvo*
soy milk - *leche de soya*
soy products - *productos de soya*
soy sauce - *salsa de soya*
spaghetti - *espagueti*
spices - *especias*
spinach - *espinaca*
split peas - *arvejas secas*
sprouts - *brotes*
squash (winter or hard) - *ayote*
squid - *calamares*
star anis - *anís de estrella*
star apple - *caimito*
star fruit - *carambola*
strawberries - *fresas*
string beans - *vainicas*
sugar - *azúcar*
sugar substitute - *sustituto de azúcar*
sunflower seeds - *semillas girasol*
sweet pepper - *chile dulce*
sweet potato - *camote*
sweet potato, orange - *camote naranja, camote zanahoria*
sweetened condensed milk - *dulce leche*
sweetened whipped cream - *crema chantillí*
swiss chard - *acelga*
syrup - *sirope*

&ex; T &xe;

tail - *rabo, cola*
tangerine - *mandarina*
tea - *té*

tea, black - *té negro*
tea, chamomile - *té manzanilla*
tea, green - *té verde*
tea, herbal - *té de hierbas*
tea, hot - *té caliente*
tea, iced - *té frío*
tea, mint - *té menta*
tenderloin - *lomito*
tendon - *tendon*
tequila - *tequila*
texturized soy protein - *soya texturizada*
thyme - *tomillo*
tomato - *tomate*
tomato juice - *jugo de tomate*
tomato paste - *pasta de tomate*
tomato sauce - *salsa de tomate, salsa de pomodoro*
tomatoes, canned and diced - *tomates en trocitos*
tongue - *lengua*
tonic water - *tónica*
tortilla - *tortilla*
tortilla chips - *tortillas horneadas de maíz*
tortillas, corn - *tortillas de maíz*
tortillas, wheat - *tortillas de trigo*
tripe - *mondongo*
trout - *trucha*
tuna - *atún*
turbot - *rodaballo, rapante*
turkey - *pavo*
turkey breast, frozen - *pechuga de pavo congelada*
turkey ham - *jamón de pavo*
turkey ham, smoked - *jamón de pavo ahumado*
turkey sausage - *salchicha de pavo*
turkey, whole, raw - *pavo entero crudo*
turkey, whole, roasted - *pavo entero asado al horno*
turmeric - *cúrcuma*

turnip - *nabo*

❧ U-V ❧

vanilla extract - *vainilla, esencia de vainilla*
vanilla bean - *vaina de vainilla*
veal - *ternera*
veal cutlet - *carne para milanesa de ternera*
veal roast - *posta de res de ternera*
veal, eye of round - *mano de piedra de res de ternera*
veal, leg of - *pierna de res de ternera*
veal, loin - *lomo de res de ternera*
veal, shank - *jarrete de ternera*
veal, short ribs - *costillas de res de ternera*
veal, sirloin - *sirloin de res de ternera*
veal, T bone - *T bone de res de ternera*
veal, tenderloin - *lomito de res de ternera*
vegetable broth - *caldo de vegetales*
vegetable pear - *chayote*
vegetables - *vegetales, legumbres, verduras*
vermouth - *vermut*
vinegar, balsamic - *vinagre balsámico*
vinegar, red wine - *vinagre de vino tinto*
vinegar, rice - *vinagre de arroz*
vinegar, white wine - *vinagre de vino blanco*
vodka - *vodka*

❧ W-Z ❧

walnuts - *nuez, nueces*
water - *agua*
water apple - *manzana de agua*
water, bottled - *agua embotellada, una botella de agua*
watermelon - *sandía*
wheat - *trigo*

wheat flour - *harina de trigo*
wheat tortilla - *tortilla de harina*
whipped cream - *nata montada, crema batida*
whipping cream - *crema dulce*
whisky - *wiski, whisky*
whole grain flour - *harina integral*
wine - *vino*
wine, Bordeaux - *vino de bordeos*
wine, Burgundy - *vino Borgoña*
wine, port - *oporto*
wine, red - *vino tinto*
wine, rosé - *vino rosado*
wine, sparkling - *vino espumoso*
wine, sweet - *vino dulce*
wine, white - *vino blanco*
with ice - *con hielo*
Worsteshire sauce - *salsa inglesa*
yeast - *levadura*
yogurt - *yogur*
yogurt, plain - *yogur natural*
yuca - *yuca, yucca*
zucchini - *zucchinni, zapallito, calabazin, zukini*

Food Dictionary Alphabetical - *Spanish* to English

❧ A ❧

abadejo - haddock
aceite - oil
aceite de ajonjolí - sesame oil
aceite de canola - canola oil
aceite de maiz - corn oil
aceite de oliva - olive oil
aceite de oliva extra virgen - extra virgen olive oil
aceite de palma - oil, palm
aceite de sésamo - sesame oil
aceite de soya - soy oil
aceite de vegetal - vegetable oil
aceite en spray - cooking spray
aceite para rociar - cooking spray
aceitunas, olivas - olives
acelga - swiss chard
achicoria - radicchio
achiote - annatto seed, ground or in a paste
aderezo - dressing
agua - water
agua de pipa - coconut water
agua embotellada - bottled water
agua mineral con gas - mineral water, sparkling
agua mineral sin gas - mineral water, flat
agua potable - drinking water

aguacate - avocado
ajo - garlic
alas de pollo - chicken wings
albahaca - basil
albahaca de limón - lemon basil
albahaca morada - purple basil
albaricoque - apricot
albaricoques secos - apricots, dried
albóndigas - meatballs
alcachofa - artichoke
alcaparras - capers
alimentos congelados - frozen food
alimentos enlatados - canned foods
alimentos preparados - prepared foods
alipego de res - beef, flank steak
alitas de pollo - chicken wings
almeja - clam
almendras - almonds
anchoa - anchovy
anguila - eel
anís de estrella - star anis
anona - custard apple
aperitivo - aperitif
apio - celery
arándanos secos - cranberries, dried
arándanos, arándanos rojos - cranberries
arándanos azules - blueberries
arándanos deshidratados - cranberries, dried
arenque - herring
arrachera de res - beef, inside skirt steak
arroz - rice
arroz "arborrio" - arborrio rice
arroz arborio, arroz para risotto - rice, arborio
arroz de grano corto - rice, short grain
arroz de grano largo - rice, long grain

arroz integral - whole grain brown rice
arroz para risotto - arborrio rice
arúgula - arugula
arvejas secas - split peas
arvejas verdes - peas
asado de cordero - lamb, breast
atún - tuna
avellana - hazelnut
avena - oatmeal
avena "al minuto" - oats, quick cooking
avena integral - oats, whole grain
avena mosh - oats, quick cooking
avena "rapido" - oats, quick cooking
aves de corral - poultry
ayote - squash (winter or hard)
azafrán - saffron
azúcar - sugar
azúcar blanco de plantación molido - confectioners sugar, glazing sugar, powdered sugar
azúcar en polvo - powdered sugar, confectioners sugar, glazing sugar
azúcar glacé - glazing sugar, confectioners sugar, powdered sugar
azúcar moreno - brown sugar

☙ B-C ❧

bacalao - cod
banano - banana
barra de mantequilla - butter, stick of
batido - smoothie or milkshake
batido de chocolate - chocolate milkshake
bebida - drink
bebidas - beverages
berenjena - eggplant
bicarbonato, bicarbonato de sodio - baking soda
bistec de res - beef steak

bok choy - Bok Choy
bolita de res - beef, knuckle (Sirloin tip)
brócoli - broccoli
brotes - sprouts
caballa - mackerel
cacao - cocoa
cachetes - cheeks
cacho de paleta de res - beef, mock tender
cacho de vuelta de lomo de res - beef, tri-tip
café - coffee
café tueste oscuro - coffee, dark roast
café chorreado - coffee, made in traditional Tico drip style
café con leche - coffee with milk
café descafeinado - coffee, decaffeinated
café instantáneo - coffee, instant
café molido - coffee, ground
café negro - coffee, black
caimito - star apple
calabaza - pumpkin
calabazin - zucchini
calamares - squid
caldo de pollo - chicken broth
caldo de res - beef broth
caldo de vegetales - vegetable broth
camarón, camarónes - shrimp
camote - sweet potato
camote naranja, camote zanahoria - sweet potato, orange
canela - cinnamon
cangrejo - crab
carambola - star fruit
cardamomo - cardamon
carne - meat
carne de cerdo - pork
carne mechada - shredded meat
carne mechada de res - beef, shredded

carne molida de cerdo - pork, ground
carne molida de res - beef, ground
carne molida de res corriente - beef, ground, regular
carne molida de res especial - beef, ground, prime
carne molida de pollo - chicken, ground
carne para milanesa de ternera - veal cutlet
carnes - meats
cas - sour guava
catchup - ketchup
caviar - caviar
cebada - barley
cebolla - onion
cebolla morada - purple onion
cebollinos - scallions
cecina de res - beef, outside skirt steak
cerdo - pork
cereales - cereals
cereza - cherry
cerveza - beer
cerveza de barril or cerveza cruda - beer, draught
cerveza de importación - beer, imported
cerveza michelada - beer with lime juice
cerveza negra - beer, dark
cerveza rubia - lager
cerveza sin alcohol - beer, non-alcoholic
champán - champagne
champaña - champagne
champiñon pequeño - button mushroom
chayote - vegetable pear
chicharrones - pork, cracklings (fried pork belly or fried pork rinds)
chile dulce - sweet pepper
chile jalapeño - jalapeño
chile morrón - bell pepper
chile picante - hot chili pepper
chiles chipotle en salsa de adobo - chipotle chiles in adobo sauce

chirivía - parsnip
chocolate caliente - hot chocolate
chorizo - Mexican syle sausage
chorreadas - corn pancakes
chuleta de cerdo - pork, chop
chuleta de cerdo ahumada - pork, chop, smoked
chuletas de cordero - lamb chops
chyves - chives
ciruela - plum
ciruelas pasas - prunes
clara de huevo - egg white
clavos de olor - cloves
coca - Coke, cola
coco - coconut
coco rallado - coconut, shredded
cóctel - cocktail
cola de buey - oxtail
coles de Bruselas - Brussels sprouts
coliflor - cauliflower
comino - cumin
con hielo - with ice
coñac - brandy
condimentos - condiments, seasonings
conejo - rabbit
confites - candy
congelados - frozen foods
congrio - eel
corazon - heart
corazón de paleta de res - beef, shoulder clod
corazones de alcachofa - artichoke hearts
cordero - lamb
corona de... - crown roast of...
corteza variada de fruta - mixed fruit peel
corvina - sea bass
cosas de picar - snack food

costilla de cerdo baby back - pork, baby back spare ribs
costilla de res - beef, back ribs or short ribs
costillas de cerdo - pork, spare ribs
costillas de cordero - lamb, ribs
costillas de res de ternera - veal, short ribs
crema batida - whipped cream
crema chantillí - Chantilly cream, sweetened whipped cream
crema de coco - coconut cream (sweetened)
crema dulce - whipping cream
cremor tartaro - cream of tartar
crutons - croutons
cuarto delantero - forequarter cuts
cuarto trasero - hindquarter cuts
cubitos de res - beef, cubes or pieces
culantro - cilantro, coriander
culantro coyote - culantro
cúrcuma - turmeric
curry - curry
cús-cús - cous cous

❧ D-F ❧

dedos de señora - lady fingers
Delmonico con hueso - beef, ribeye bone-in or cowboy steak
diente de ajo - garlic clove
dorado - mahi mahi
dulce de leche - caramel sauce, milk-based
dulce leche - sweetened condensed milk
dulces - candy, sweets
echalotes - shallots
edulcorante artificial - artificial sweetener
elote - corn on the cob
embutidos - processed packaged meat
en las rocas - on the rocks
endulzante artificial - artificial sweetener

eneldo - dill
escarola - endive
escombro - mackerel
espadilla de cordero - lamb, shoulder chop
espagueti - spaghetti
espárragos - asparagus
especias - spices
espinaca - spinach
falda de cerdo - pork, flank steak
falda de res - beef, skirt steak
fécula de maíz - corn starch
fideos - noodles
filete de flanco - beef, flank steak
filete de jamón - ham steak
filete de res - beef, fillet
frambuesas - raspberries
fresas - strawberries
frijoles - beans
frijoles blancos - beans, white or navy
frijoles de lima - lima beans
frijoles enteros - beans, whole
frijoles molidos - beans, refried
frijoles nacidos - bean sprouts
frijoles negros - beans, black
frijoles rojos - beans, red
frijoles de soya - beans, soy
frisee - frisée
fruta - fruit
frutas - fruits
frutas secas - dried fruits

❧ G-I ❧

galletas - cookies or crackers
galletas soda - soda crackers

gallina - hen
gallinilla - beef, tri-tip
gallo - rooster
gamba - prawn
garbanzos - chick peas
gaseoso - soft drinks, soda
gelatina - gelatin
gelatina sin sabor - gelatin, unflavored
ginebra - gin
ginger ale, gin - ginger ale
granadilla - a type of passion fruit
granos - grains
granos de café - coffee beans
grissini - breadsticks
guanábana - soursop
guaro (Cacique) - Costa Rican sugar cane liquor
guayaba - guava
guisantes verdes - peas
hamburguesa - hamburger
hamburguesa con queso - cheeseburger
harina - flour
harina común - flour, all-purpose
harina de repostería - flour, pastry or cake
harina de trigo - wheat flour
harina integral - whole grain flour
helado - ice cream
hielo - ice
hierbabuena - peppermint
hierbas - herbs
hierbas provenzales - herbs de provence
hígado - liver
hígado de res - beef, liver
hígados de pollo - chicken livers
higos - figs
hinojo - fennel

hoja de laurel - bay leaf
hojitas de hierbabuena - peppermint leaves
hojuelas de avena integral - oats, rolled
hongos - mushrooms
huesos - bones
huesos para sopa - soup bones
huevos - eggs
ice - hielo
ingredientes para hornear - baking ingredients

ঌ J-K ক

jalea - jelly
jalea de arándanos - cranberry sauce, jellied, canned
jamón - ham
jamón ahumado - ham, smoked
jamón de pavo - turkey ham
jamón de pavo ahumado - turkey ham, smoked
jamón prosciutto - prosciutto
jarrete de cordero - lamb shank
jarrete de res - beef, shank
jarrete de ternera - veal, shank
jengibre en polvo - ginger, ground
jerez - sherry
jocote - Jamaican plum
jugo - juice
jugo de fruta - fruit juice
jugo de limón - lemon juice
jugo de manzana - apple juice
jugo de naranja - orange juice
jugo de naranja ricién exprimido - orange juice, freshly squeezed
jugo de tomate - tomato juice
jugo de toronja - grapefruit juice
kale - kale
kétchup - ketchup

kiwi - kiwi

◈ L ◈

lácteos - dairy
langosta - lobster
lanzas de espárragos - asparagus spears
lardo - lard
lasaña - lasagna
leche - milk
leche agria - buttermilk (literally "sour milk")
leche condensada - milk, condensed
leche de almendras - almond milk
leche de cabra - goat's milk
leche de coco - coconut milk
leche de oveja - sheep's milk
leche de soya - soy milk
leche de vaca - cow's milk
leche descremada - milk, skimmed
leche deslactosada - milk, lactose-free
leche en polvo - milk, powdered
leche evaporada - evaporated milk
leche fría - milk, cold
leche semi-descremada 2% grasa - milk, reduced-fat (2%)
lechuga - lettuce
lechuga americana - lettuce, iceburg
lechuga romana - lettuce, romaine
lecitina de soya en polvo - soy lecithin
legumbres - vegetables
lengua - tongue
lentejas - lentils
levadura - yeast
licor - liquor
licor de café - coffee liqueur
licor de menta - creme de menthe

licor de naranja - orange liqueur
licuado - smoothie
limón - lime
limón mandarino - mandarin lime
limonada - lemonade
linaza molida - flax seeds, ground
lomito - tenderloin
lomito de cerdo - pork, tenderloin
lomito de entraña de res - beef, hanging tender
lomito de res - beef, tenderloin
lomito de res con hueso - beef, tenderloin, bone-in
lomito de res de ternera - veal, tenderloin
lomo - loin
lomo ancho de res - beef, strip loin
lomo de aguja de res - beef, chuck roll
lomo de cerdo - pork, boneless tenderloin
lomo de paleta de res - beef, top blade
lomo de res de ternera - veal, loin
lomo Delmonico - beef, ribeye (lip on) roll
lomo entero de res - beef, ribeye (lip on) roll

❧ M ☙

macadamias - macademia nuts
macarela - mackerel
macarrón - macaroni
maicena - corn starch
maíz - corn
maíz cáscara - hominy
maíz dulce - corn, sweet
maíz dulce entero enlatados - corn, canned, sweet
mamón chino - rambutan, lychee
mandarina - tangerine
mango - mango
maní - peanuts

manitas de cerdo - pigs feet
mano de piedra - beef, gooseneck
mano de piedra de res - beef, eye of round
mano de piedra de res de ternera - veal, eye of round
manteca - lard
manteca de cerdo - pork, lard
mantequilla - butter
mantequilla baja en grasa - butter, low-fat
manzana - apple
manzana de agua - water apple
maracuyá - passion fruit
marañon - cashew fruit
margarina - margarine
mariscos - seafood
mayonesa - mayonnaise
mejillones - mussels
mejorana - marjoram
melaza - molasses
melocotón - peach
melocotones en conserva - peaches, canned
melón - cantaloupe
melón de casaba - casaba melon
menta - mint
menudo de pollo - chicken organs, necks & feet (mixed)
mermelada - jam
mermelada de piña - pineapple marmalade or jam
miel de abeja - honey
miel de maple - maple syrup
milanesa - cutlet, thinly cut meat or poultry
milanesa de cerdo - pork, cutlet
milanesa de pollo - chicken cutlets (or pounded breasts)
milanesa de res - beef, cutlets
molida de cerdo - pork, ground
mollejas - gizzards
mondongo - tripe

moras - blackberries
morcilla de cerdo - blood sausage
morro de res - beef, hump
mortadela - bologna
mostaza - mustard
mostaza china - Chinese cabbage
mostaza Dijon - Dijon mustard
mostaza en polvo - mustard, dry, ground
muslito de muslo - chicken drumsticks
muslos de alas - chicken drummettes
muslos de pollo - chicken thighs
muslos de pollo enteros - chicken leg quarters

❧ N-O ❧

nabo - turnip
nance, nanzi - shoemaker fruit
naranja - orange
nata montada - whipped cream
natilla - sour cream
nectarina - nectarine
níspero - Japanese plum
nueces - walnuts, nuts in general
nueces mixtas, nueces mezcladas, nueces variadas - mixed nuts
nuez moscada - nutmeg
nuez moscada en polvo - nutmeg, dry, grated
oporto - wine, port
orégano - oregano
osobuco, ossobuco de res - beef, shank, cross-cut
ossobuco de res de ternera - osso buco (cross-cut veal shanks)
ostra - oyster
ovejas, carneros - sheep

❧ P ❧

pak choi - Bok Choy
paleta de res - beef, chuck shoulder
palitos de pan - breadsticks
palmitos - hearts of palm
palomitas de maíz - popcorn
pan - bread
pan de masa madre - bread, sourdough
pan rallado - bread crumbs
pan rebanado - sliced bread
papa - potato
papas tostadas - potato chips
papaya - papaya
paprika - paprika
pargo rojo - red snapper
pasas - raisins
pasta de hojaldre - puff pastry
pasta de tomate - tomato paste
pasta enriquecida - enriched pasta
pasta filo - filo pastry
pasta fresca - pasta, fresh
pastrame de res - pastrami
patas de cerdo - pigs feet
pate - paté
pato - duck
pavo - turkey
pavo entero asado al horno - turkey, whole, roasted
pavo entero crudo - turkey, whole, raw
pecanas - pecans
pecho curado de res - corned beef
pecho de res - beef, brisket
pechuga de pavo congelada - turkey breast, frozen
pechuga entera - chicken breasts on the bone with ribs
pechuga filete - chicken breasts, boneless & skinless

pechugas de pollo - chicken breasts
pejibaye - peach palm
pepinillo en rodajas - pickle slices
pepinillos - pickles
pepino - cucumber
pera - pear
perejil - parsley
perejil plano - Italian flat leaf parsley
perro caliente - hot dog
pescado - fish
petit pois - peas
pierna de cerdo - pork, leg
pierna de cerdo con piel - pork, leg with skin
pierna de cordero - lamb, leg of
pierna de res de ternera - veal, leg of
pierna de... - back leg of...
pimienta blanca - pepper, white
pimienta cayena - pepper, cayenne
pimienta negra - pepper, black
piña - pineapple
piñones - pine nuts
pipa - coconut, green
pistacho - pistachio
plátano - plantain
plátano verde - plantain, green
plumas, pasta penne - pasta, penne
pollo - chicken
pollo entero limpio - chicken, whole
polvo para hornear - baking powder
porter house de res - beef, Porterhouse steak
posta de cerdo - pork, roast
posta de cuarto de res - beef, top round, inside round, or rump
posta de paleta de cerdo - pork, shoulder roast
posta de paleta de res - beef, shoulder clod
posta de ratón trasero de res - beef, heel of round or gooseneck

posta de res de ternera - veal roast
postre - dessert
productos de soya - soy products
productos enlatados - canned goods
productos lácteos - dairy products
pudin instantaneo - pudding, instant
puerro - leek
pulpo - octopus
punta de jamon - ham end
punta de solomo de res - beef, top sirloin cap steak

ཀ Q-R ঞ

queque - cake
queque de zanahoria - carrot cake
queso - cheese
queso "cottage" - cottage cheese
queso asiago - asiago cheese
queso azul - blue cheese
queso bocconcini - mozzarella, baby
queso brie frances - brie
queso camembert frances - Camembert
queso cheddar - cheddar cheese
queso crema, queso Philadelphia - cream cheese
queso de cabra - goat cheese
queso de oveja - sheep's milk cheese
queso de soya - soy cheese
queso desmenuzado - cheese, shredded
queso feta - feta cheese
queso fresco tierno - fresh soft cheese
queso gouda - gouda
queso mozarela - mozzarella
queso parmesano - parmesan cheese
queso pecorino - Pecorino romano
queso ricotta - ricotta

queso semiduro - cheese, mild, semisoft
quinada - quinine water
rábano, rabano rojo - radish
rabo de buey - oxtail
rabo de res - beef, tail
rabo, cola - tail
raíz de jengibre - ginger root
ramita de canela - cinnamon stick
rapante - turbot
ratón delantero de res con hueso - beef, foreshank, bone-in
ratón trasero de res con hueso - beef, hind shank, bone-in
ratón trasero de res sin hueso - beef, hind shank, boneless
rayadura de limón - lemon zest
refresco con agua - fruit drink with water base
refresco con leche - fruit drink with milk base
refrigerados - refrigerated foods
remolacha - beet
repollo morado - cabbage, purple
repollo verde - cabbage, green
res - beef
rib eye de res - beef, ribeye (lip on) roll
riñon - kidney
riñones de res - beef, kidneys
rodaballo - turbot
romero - rosemary
ron - rum
ron con coca - rum and coke
rúcula - arugula

❧ S ❧

sal - salt
sal ahumada - salt, smoked
sal del mar - sea salt
sal del mar Himalaya - Himalayan sea salt

sal marina - sea salt
sal marina Himalaya - Himalayan sea salt
salchicha - sausage, hot dog
salchicha de pavo - turkey sausage
salchicha desayuno - breakfast sausage
salchicha frankfurter - hot dog
salchichón - sausage
salami - salami
salmón - salmon
salsa - sauce, salsa
salsa Lizano (used in gallo pinto) - Lizano sauce
salsa de pomodoro - tomato sauce
salsa de soya - soy sauce
salsa de tomate - ketchup
salsa de tomate - tomato sauce
salsa inglesa - Worsteshire sauce
salvia - sage
sandía - watermelon
sardina - sardine
sazonador de hierbas italianas - Italian seasoning
sazonadores - seasonings
semillas - seeds
semillas ajonjoli - sesame seeds
semillas de apio - celery seeds
semillas de hinojo - fennel seeds
semillas de linaza - flax seeds
semillas de marañón - cashews
semillas girasol - sunflower seeds
sémola - semolina
sesos - brains
shoulder - paleta
sidra - cider
sin alcohol - non-alcoholic
sirloin de res de ternera - veal, sirloin
sirope - syrup

sirope de maple - maple syrup
Solomo de res - beef, bottom round or gooseneck
sopa enlatada - soup, canned
soya texturizada - texturized soy protein
spray de cocina - cooking spray
sustituto de azúcar - sugar substitute

❧ T-U ❧

T bone de res de ternera - veal, T bone
tapa de dulce molida - cane sugar, unrefined, ground
t-bone de res - beef, T-bone steak
té - tea
té caliente - tea, hot
té de hierbas - tea, herbal
té frío - iced tea
té manzanilla - chamomile tea
té menta - tea, mint
té negro - tea, black
té verde - green tea
tendon - tendon
tequila - tequila
ternera - veal
tocineta ahumada - bacon, smoked
tocineta, tocino - bacon
tomate - tomato
tomates cherry - cherry tomatoes
tomates en trocitos - tomatoes, canned and diced
tomillo - thyme
tónica - tonic water
toronja - grapefruit
tortilla - tortilla
tortilla de harina - flour tortilla
tortilla de maíz - corn tortilla
tortillas de trigo - tortillas, wheat

tortillas horneadas de maíz - tortilla chips
trigo - wheat
trocitos de res - beef, cubes or pieces
trocitos de... - chunks of...
trucha - trout
uchuva - cape gooseberry, golden berry
una botella de agua - a bottle of water
uvas - grapes
uvas moradas - grapes, purple
uvas sin semillas - grapes, seedless
uvas verdes - grapes, green

❧ V-Z ❧

vaina de vainilla - vanilla bean
vainicas - green beans (string beans)
vainicas chinas - Chinese snow peas
vainilla, esencia de vainilla - vanilla extract
vegetales - vegetables
verduras - vegetables
vermut - vermouth
vieira - scallop
vinagre balsámico - balsamic vinegar
vinagre de arroz - vinegar, rice
vinagre de vino blanco - vinegar, white wine
vinagre de vino tinto - vinegar, red wine
vino - wine
vino blanco - wine, white
vino Borgoña - wine, Burgundy
vino de bordeos - wine, Bordeaux
vino dulce - wine, sweet
vino espumoso - wine, sparkling
vino rosado - wine, rosé
vino tinto - wine, red
vodka - vodka

vuelta de lomo de res - beef, top sirloin butt, center cut sirloin
whisky escocés - scotch
wiski, whisky - whisky
yema de huevo - egg yolk
yogur - yogurt
yogur natural - yogurt, plain
yuca, yucca - yuca
zacate de limón - lemongrass
zanahoria - carrot
zapallito - zucchini
zucchinni - zucchini
zukini - zucchini

Things You Find in the Kitchen - *Cosas en la Cocina* (English to *Spanish*)

aluminum foil - *papel de aluminio*
bag - *bolsa*
baking dish - *recipiente para horno*
baking pan - *molde*
barbecue grate - *parrilla*
basket - *canasta*
blender - *licuadora*
bottle - *botella*
bowl - *tazón*
carafe - *garrafa*
casserole, saucepan - *cazuela*
cast iron - *hierro fundido*
chopsticks - *palitos chinos*
cocktail shaker - *coctelera*
coffee pot - *cafetera*
container - *recipiente*
cooler - *hielera*
cork - *corcho*
corkscrew - *sacacorchos*
cup - *taza*
cutlery - *cubiertos*
cutting board - *tabla*
dinnerware, dishes - *trastos*
dishwasher - *lavadora de platos*
double boiler - *baño Maria*

electric frying-pan - *sartén eléctrica*
food processor - *procesador de alimentos*
fork - *tenedor*
freezer - *congeladora*
frying-pan, skillet - *sartén*
glass - *vaso*
glass bowl - *tazón de vidrio*
grill pan - *plancha*
hotplate - *plantilla*
juicer, juice squeezer - *extractor de jugo, el exprimidor*
kettle - *hervidor de agua*
kitchen - *cocina*
kitchen twine - *pabilo*
knife - *cuchillo*
large spoon, ladle - *cucharón*
lid or cover - *tapa, tapadera*
microwave oven - *horno de microondas*
mixer - *batidora*
napkin - *servilleta*
oven - *horno*
paper towels - *toallas de papel*
parchment paper - *papel parchment*
pastry bag - *manga de pastelera*
pitcher - *pichel*
plastic wrap - *papel plástico*
plate - *plato*
pot, stew pot - *olla*
pressure cooker - *olla de presión*
rack - *escurridor*
refrigerator - *refrigeradora*
rolling pin - *rodillo*
saucepan - *olla, ollita*
saucer - *platillo*
scales - *pesas, romanas*
scraper - *raspador*

serving spoon - *cuchara grande para servir, cucharón*
sieve - *tamiz*
skewer - *pincho*
small saucepan - *cacito*
soup spoon - *cuchara sopera*
spatula - *espátula*
stove - *estufa, cocina*
strainer - *colador*
straws, drinking - *pajillas para beber*
table - *mesa*
tablecloth - *mantel*
tablespoon - *cucharada (cda.)*
teaspoon - *cucharadita (cdita.)*
toaster - *tostadora*
toothpicks, wooden toothpicks - *palillos, palillos de madera*
tray - *bandeja*
utensils - *utensilios*
water bath - *baño Maria*
wax paper - *papel encerado*
wine bucket - *balde (para vino)*
wine glass - *copa*
wooden skewers - *pinchos de madera*
wooden spoon - *cuchara de madera*

Cosas en la Cocina - Things You Find in the Kitchen (*Spanish* to English)

balde (para vino) - wine bucket
bandeja - tray
baño Maria - double boiler or water bath
batidora - mixer
bolsa - bag
botella - bottle
cacerola - saucepan
cacito - small saucepan
cafetera - coffee pot
canasta - basket
cazuela - casserole, saucepan
cda. - tablespoon (*cucharada*)
cdita. - teaspoon (*cucharadita*)
cocina - kitchen
coctelera - cocktail shaker
colador - strainer
congeladora - freezer
copa - wine glass
corcho - cork
cubiertos - cutlery
cuchara de madera - wooden spoon
cuchara grande para servir - serving spoon
cuchara sopera - soup spoon
cucharada (cda.) - tablespoon
cucharadita (cdita.) - teaspoon

cucharón - serving spoon, ladle
cuchillo - knife
escurridor - rack
espátula - spatula
estufa, cocina - stove
exprimidor - juicer, juice squeezer
extractor de jugo - juicer, juice squeezer
garrafa - carafe
hervidor de agua - kettle
hielera - cooler
hierro fundido - cast iron
horno - oven
horno de microondas - microwave oven
lavadora de platos - dishwasher
licuadora - blender
manga de pastelera - pastry bag
mantel - tablecloth
mesa - table
molde - baking pan
olla - stew pot or sauce pan
olla de presión - pressure cooker
pabilo - kitchen twine
pajillas para beber - straws, drinking
palillos - toothpicks
palillos de madera - wooden toothpicks
palitos chinos - chopsticks
papel de aluminio - aluminum foil
papel encerado - wax paper
papel parchment - parchment paper
papel plástico - plastic wrap
parrilla - barbecue grate
pesas, romanas - scales
pichel - pitcher
pincho - skewer
pinchos de madera - wooden skewers

plancha - grill pan

plantilla - hotplate

platillo - saucer

plato - plate

procesador de alimentos - food processor

raspador - scraper

recipiente - container

recipiente para horno - baking dish

refrigeradora - refrigerator

rodillo - rolling pin

sacacorchos - corkscrew

sartén - frying-pan, skillet

sartén eléctrica - electric frying-pan

servilleta - napkin

tabla - cutting board

tamiz - sieve

tapa, tapadera - lid or cover

taza - cup

tazón - bowl

tazón de vidrio - glass bowl

tenedor - fork

toallas de papel - paper towels

tostadora - toaster

trastos - dinnerware, dishes

utensilios - utensils

vaso - glass

Glossary of Cooking Terms and Helpful Adjectives - *Glosario de Términos de Cocina y Adjetivos Útiles* (English to *Spanish*)

a bottle of... - *una botella de...*
a can of... - *una lata de...*
a carton of... - *un cartón de*
a crack or split - *rajadura*
a few (some) minutes - *unos minutos*
a few (some) seconds - *unos segundos*
a marinade, pickle, or brine - *escabeche*
a package of... - *un paquete de...*
accompanied - *acompañados/as*
acidic, sour - *ácido/a*
addition - *adición*
advanced - *avanzado/a*
alcoholic - *alcohólico, con alcohol*
alimentos congelados - *frozen food*
alternating - *alternando/a*
appetizer or snack - *bocadito or bocadillo*
approximately - *aproximadamente*
Are you hungry? - *¿Tiene hambre?*
around - *alrededor*
asparagus spears - *lanzas de espárragos*
assorted, an assortment - *surtido/a*
atop, on top of - *encima*
back - *espalda*
back to back - *espalda con espalda*

bad - *malo/a*
baked - *horneado/a*
baked or roasted in the oven - *al horno*
baked potato - *papa al horno*
bakery - *panadería*
ball - *bola*
barbecue grate - *parrilla*
barbecued - *a la barbacoa*
batter - *batido para rebozar*
beat the eggs - *bata los huevos*
beaten, whipped - *batido/a*
beverages - *bebidas*
bitter, unsweetened - *amargo/a*
bittersweet, sweet & sour - *agridulce*
black pepper freshly ground - *pimienta negra molida fresca*
bland, flavorless - *sin sabor, soso/a*
blended - *mezclado/a*
body - *cuerpo*
boiled - *hervido/a*
boiling - *hirviendo/a*
boiling water - *agua hirviendo*
bones - *huesos*
bottom, base - *fondo*
box or package - *caja*
breaded - *empanizado/a*
breakfast - *desayuno*
briefly - *brevemente*
bring to a boil - *rompa el hervor*
brochette - *brocheta*
broth - *caldo*
brown on both sides - *dore por ambos lados*
browned - *dorado/a*
bubbles - *burbujas*
bulb - *bulbo*
bunch or cluster of grapes - *racimo de uvas*

buns - *bollos*
burnt - *quemado/a*
butcher - *carnicero*
butcher shop, meat market - *carnicería*
cake - *queque*
can of... - *lata de...*
canned - *enlatado/a*
caramelized - *caramelizado/a*
caramelized onions - *cebollas caramelizadas*
carbohydrate - *carbohidrato*
carefully - *cuidadosamente*
charbroiled - *en churrasco*
charcoal grilled - *al carbón, a las brasas*
Cheers! To your health! - *¡Salud!*
cheese sticks - *palitos de queso*
cheesecake - *pastel de queso*
chewy - *se tiene que masticar mucho*
cholesterol - *colesterol*
chopped in small pieces - *picado/a en trozos finos*
chopped, minced - *picado/a*
cloves of garlic - *dientes de ajo*
cold - *frío/a*
condensed - *condensado/a*
consistency - *consistencia*
continue cooking - *siga cocinando*
cooked - *cocido/a*
cooked au gratin - *gratinado/a*
cooked in very little water (literally, "sweaty") - *sudado/a*
cool place - *sitio frío*
cool - *fresco/a*
corrugated, grooved - *corrugado/a, acanalado/a*
course, dish - *plato (de una comida)*
covered - *cubierto/a, tapado/a*
cream - *crema*
creamy - *cremoso/a*

crepes - *crepas*
crown of... - *corona de...*
crumbled or shredded - *desmenuzado/a*
crunchy, crispy - *crujiente*
crushed - *machacado/a*
crushed, or ground - *triturado/a*
crystalized - *cristalizado/a*
cubes or dice of... - *cubitos de...*
cubes or dice of... - *dados de...*
cut in half - *cortado/a por la mitad*
cut into cubes - *en cubos*
cut or chopped - *cortado/a*
dash or pinch (of seasoning) - *pizca*
deboned - *deshuesado/a*
defatted, skim - *desgrasado/a*
defrosted - *descongelado/a*
dehydrated - *deshidratado/a*
delicious - *delicioso/a*
delicious (literally "rich") - *rico/a*
dense - *denso/a*
desired - *deseado/a*
dessert - *postre*
difficult - *difícil*
dinner - *cena*
dissolved - *disuelto/a*
divided - *partido/a*
dough - *masa*
drained - *escurrido/a*
drained weight - *peso escurrido*
dressing, seasoning - *aderezo*
dried - *seco/a*
droplets - *gotitas*
drops - *gotas*
drying - *secando/a*
easy - *fácil*

edge or border - *orilla*

empty or hollow - *vacío/a*

Enjoy your meal! - *¡Buen Provecho!*

enjoyable, nice - *agradable*

entire or whole - *entero/a*

envelopes of... - *sobres de...*

evaporated - *evaporado/a*

excellent - *excelente*

fast food - *comida rápida*

fillet of... - *filete de...*

finely chopped - *finamente cortado/a*

finely chopped - *picado/a fino or finamente picado/a*

finished to your liking (your taste) - *al término de su gusto*

fire or heat - *fuego*

fizzy - *gaseoso/a*

flaked - *en pedacitos*

flavors - *sabores*

foam - *espuma*

following, next - *siguiente*

food allergy - *alergia alimentaria*

food or meal - *comida*

for a couple of minutes - *por un par de minutos*

fragrant - *bien aromático/a*

french fries - *papas fritas*

fresh - *fresco/a*

freshly squeezed - *recién exprimido*

fried - *frito/a*

fried or sauted with garlic - *al ajillo*

froth the egg whites to peaks (literally "to snow the clear") - *nevar las claras*

frothy, bubbly - *espumoso/a*

frozen - *congelado/a*

fruity - *afrutado/a*

full, generous - *generoso/a*

gently - *gentilmente*

gently (literally "with care") - *con cuidado*
giving it... - *dándole*
glazed - *glaseado/a, con glasé*
good - *bueno/a*
gooey, viscous - *viscoso/a*
grains or beans, as in coffee beans - *granos*
gram - *gramo (g.)*
grated - *rallado/a*
grated peel or rind - *ralladura*
grease and flour (a pan) - *engrase y enharine*
grease or fat - *grasa*
greased - *engrasado/a*
greasy - *grasiento*
grilled - *en parilla*
grilled on a grill pan, broiled - *a la plancha*
grilled on an open grate - *a la parrilla*
grilled or roasted over a wood fire - *a la leña*
grooved, corrugated - *acanalado/a, corrugado/a*
ground - *molido/a*
half - *medio/a, mitad*
handful or bunch - *manojo*
hard, tough - *duro/a*
hard-boiled egg - *huevo duro*
hash - *picadillo*
head of garlic - *cabeza de ajo*
healthy diet - *dieta saludable*
heaping tablespoons - *cucharadas colmadas, cucharadas coperas*
heat-resistant, oven-proof - *refractario*
heavy, weighty - *pesado/a*
herbs - *hierbas*
hole - *hueco*
homemade - *casero/a*
homogenous - *homogénea*
hot - *caliente*
hour - *hora*

ice - *hielo*
ice cubes - *hielo en cubitos*
if you desire - *si lo desea*
in half - *a la mitad, por la mitad*
inches - *pulgadas*
ingredients - *ingredientes*
intermediate - *intermedio/a*
internal temperature of... - *temperatura interna de...*
juicy - *jugoso/a*
julienne - *juliana*
julienned, cut into thin strips - *en juliana*
junk food - *comida basura*
kilogram - *kilogramo (kilo, kg.)*
lactose-free - *deslactosado/a*
large - *grande*
larger - *mas grande*
lastly - *por ultimo*
layer - *capa*
leaf or sheet - *hoja*
leftovers - *sobras*
lemon zest - *ralladura de limón*
level of complexity - *nivel de complejidad*
level of difficulty - *nivel de dificultad*
light - *ligero/a*
lightly oiled - *levemente aceitado/a*
liquid - *liquido/a*
liquified, blended - *licuado/a*
little by little - *poco a poco*
low-fat - *bajo/a en grasa*
lower the heat - *baje el fuego*
lower the intensity of the heat - *baje la intensidad del fuego*
lukewarm, tepid - *tibio/a*
lunch - *almuerzo*
luscious, delicious - *riquísimo*
marinated - *adobado/a, marinado/a*

marmalade or jam - *mermelada*
mashed - *majado/a*
mashed potatoes - *puré de papas*
meanwhile, in the meantime - *entretanto*
measurement - *medida*
meat - *carne*
meatballs - *albondigas*
medallions of... - *medallones de...*
medium - *mediano/a*
medium low (as in heat) - *medio-bajo*
medium rare - *término medio*
medium well done, as in steak - *tres cuartos*
melted - *derretido/a, fundido/a*
melted butter - *mantequilla derretida*
melted (molten) cheese - *queso fundido*
melting - *fundiendo*
menu - *menú*
menu of the day - *menú del dia*
meringue - *merengue*
mild, soft - *suave*
minutes - *minutos*
mixture - *mezcla*
must, should, ought to - *deber, deba*
non-alcoholic - *sin alcohol*
non-fat, skimmed, as in milk - *descremado/a*
not dry - *no seco*
not sufficient, underdone - *no suficiente*
number of portions - *numero de porciones*
nutrients - *nutrientes*
nutrition, nourishment - *alimentación*
on a bed of... - *sobre una cama de...*
on a high heat - *a fuego alto*
on a low heat - *a fuego lento, a fuego bajo*
on a medium heat - *a fuego medio, a fuego moderado*
on both sides - *por ambos lados*

on the point of... (when) - *a punto de...*
once - *una vez*
once cooked - *una vez cocinado/a*
organic - *organico/a*
oven - *horno*
packet or package - *paquete*
pastry or pie - *pastel*
pastry shop - *pastelería*
pickled - *encurtido/a*
pie, turnover - *empanada*
piece - *trozo*
piece or slice - *pedazo*
pieces - *piezas*
plain - *sencillo/a*
poached - *escalfado/a, pochado/a*
portion - *porción*
powdered - *en polvo*
preheated - *precalentado/a*
preparation - *preparación*
preparation time - *tiempo de preparación*
prepared - *preparado/a*
protein - *proteina*
purée - *puré*
quantity, amount - *cantidad*
quite, enough - *bastante*
rare (meat) - *poco hecho, or poco asado*
raw, undercooked - *crudo/a*
ready - *listo/a*
recipe - *receta*
reduction - *reducción*
rehydrated - *hidratado/a*
remove from the fire (take off the heat) - *sacar del fuego*
ripe, mature - *maduro/a*
roasted - *asado/a*
roll - *rollo*

rolls - *bollos*
room temperature - *temperatura ambiente*
round slice - *rodaja*
salad - *ensalada*
salt and pepper to taste - *salpimiente al gusto, sal y pimienta al gusto*
salty, salted, savory - *salado/a*
sandwich - *sándwich*
sauce - *salsa*
sautéed - *salteado/a*
scales for weighing - *balanza*
scrambled, turned over - *revuelto/a*
sear both sides - *sellar ambos lados*
seared - *sellado/a*
seasoning or flavoring - *sazón*
seasoning rub for meat - *adobo*
second course or main course - *segundo plato*
secure with wooden toothpicks - *asegure con palillos de madera*
seed - *semilla*
seedless - *sin semilla*
semi-hard - *semi-duro*
separately - *aparte*
serve immediately - *servir inmediatamente*
serves 10 persons - *para 10 personas*
sheets - *laminas*
shell, husk or rind - *cáscara*
sifted - *cernido/a*
sifted flour - *harina cernida*
singed or scorched - *chamuscado/a*
size - *tamaño*
skin-side - *el lado de la piel*
slice - *tajada, taja*
sliced - *rebanado/a*
slightly - *ligeramente*
slightly toasted - *ligeramente tostado/a*
small - *pequeño/a*

small ball - *bolita*
small holes - *huequitos*
small leaves - *hojitas*
small meatballs - *bolitas de carne*
small piece or slice - *pedacito*
small pieces, chunks - *trocitos*
small slice - *tajadita*
smaller - *mas pequeño/a*
smoked, smokey - *ahumado/a*
smooth - *liso/a*
soft, mild - *suave*
soft, pliant - *blando/a*
soft-boiled egg - *huevo blando*
some - *algunos/as, unos/as*
soup - *sopa*
sour - *agrio/a*
spicy, tangy - *picante*
spoiled - *echado a perder*
sprig, as in sprig of rosemary - *ramita*
squares - *cuadrados*
squeezed - *exprimido/a*
stale (bread) or bad (meat) - *pasado/a*
stalk, stem, or shoot - *tallo*
steamed - *al vapor*
stewed - *estofado/a, guisado/a*
stick of (butter, margarine) - *barra de...*
sticks, stalks, or stems - *palitos*
stir constantly - *revolver constantemente*
stirring continually - *revolviendo siempre*
stringy - *fibroso*
strips or shreds - *tiras*
strong - *fuerte*
stuffed, filled, or stuffing - *relleno/a*
surface area - *superficie*
sweet - *dulce*

tablespoon - *cucharada (cda.)*
take off the heat - *retire del fuego*
take out of the oven - *retire del horno*
take out of the refrigerator - *sacar de refrigeración*
taste or flavor - *sabor*
taste to check the seasoning - *pruebe la sazón*
tasty, flavorful - *sabroso/a*
teaspoon - *cucharadita (cdita.)*
temperature - *temperatura*
tender - *tierno/a*
tenderized, tender - *tenderizado/a*
thick - *grueso/a*
thickly - *gruesamente*
thickness - *grosor*
thin - *delgado/a*
thin - *ralo/a*
thin, fine - *fino/a*
time - *tiempo*
time to settle or rest - *tiempo de reposo*
to parboil - *sancochar, sancoche*
to preheat - *precalentar, precaliente*
to toast - *tostar, tuéste*
to accompany, to go well with - *acompañar, acompañe*
to add - *agregar, agregue,* or *añadir, añada*
to add or to augment - *adicionar, adicione*
to alternate - *alternar, alterne*
to arrange or line up - *disponer, disponga*
to arrange, to place - *colocar, coloque*
to ask for, to order - *pedir, pida*
to bake - *hornear, hornee*
to blanche, to whiten - *blanquear, blanquee*
to blend, beat, whip, or whisk - *batir, bata*
to boil - *hervir, hierva*
to bread something - *empanizar, empanice*
to break or burst - *romper, rompa*

to bring to the boil - *llevar a ebullición*

to brown - *dorar, dore*

to burst or crack open - *reventar, reviente*

to calculate - *calcular, calcule*

to carry or take - *llevar, lleve*

to chill or cool - *enfriar, enfrie*

to clean - *limpiar, limpie*

to cleave, slit, crack - *hender, hienda*

to close or fasten - *cerrar, cierre*

to coat or glaze (literally "to varnish") - *barnizar, barnice*

to coat, dip or bathe - *bañar, bañe*

to continue - *seguir, siga*

to cook - *cocinar, cocine*

to cook au gratin (usually covered in breadcrumbs and cheese and baked or browned in the oven) - *gratinar, gratine*

to cook or season with wine - *lamprear, lampree*

to cook, to bake - *cocer, cueza*

to correct, to rectify - *rectificar, rectifique*

to cover - *cubrir, cubra*

to cover, to put the lid on - *tapar, tape*

to crack, chip, or break - *cascar, casque*

to crumble or to flake - *desmenuzar, desmenuce*

to crush - *machacar, machaque*

to crush or grind - *triturar, triture*

to crystallize - *cristalizar, cristalice*

to curve or hollow out - *abombar, abombe*

to cut in two - *cortar en dos*

to cut into cubes, to dice - *cortar en cubos*

to cut into long slices - *cortar en longas*

to cut into quarters - *cortar en cuartos*

to cut into rings - *cortar en aros*

to cut into small discs - *cortar in rodajas*

to cut into sticks - *cortar en palitos*

to cut off the top or cap - *corte una tapita*

to cut or chop - *cortar, corte*

to decorate - *decorar, decore*
to defrost, to thaw - *descongelar, descongele*
to dehydrate - *deshidratar, deshidrate*
to dilute - *diluir, diluya*
to dine, to eat dinner/supper - *cenar, cene*
to dip in batter or eggs - *rebozar, reboce*
to dissolve - *disolver, disuelva*
to dissolve or thin in liquid - *desleír, deslía*
to divide - *dividir, divida*
to divide, to apportion, to distribute - *repartir, reparta*
to do or to make - *hacer, haga*
to double or to fold over - *doblar, doble*
to drain - *escurrir, escurra*
to dredge in flour - *pasar por harina*
to dress or season - *aderezar, aderece*
to dress or season - *condimentar, condimente*
to drink - *beber, beba*
to dry - *secar, seque*
to dump or pour - *volcar, vuelque*
to eat - *comer, coma*
to eat breakfast - *desayunar, desayune*
to empty, to hollow out, to drain - *vaciar, vacie*
to enjoy - *disfrutar, disfrute*
to extract or pull out - *extraer, extraiga (re-alpha)*
to finely chop or mince - *picar, pique*
to fold - *plegar, pliegue*
to form a ball - *formar una bola*
to form a disc - *formar un disco*
to form or shape - *formar, forme*
to freeze - *congelar, congele*
to froth or foam, to skim off - *espumar, espume*
to fry - *freír, fría*
to give something grill marks - *marque en la parilla*
to grate - *rallar, ralle*
to grease or oil - *engrasar, engrase*

to grease with oil or butter, to spread or smear - *untar, unte*

to grind or mill - *moler, muela*

to harden - *endurecer, endurezca*

to have lunch - *almorzar, almuerce*

to hydrate - *hidratar, hidrate*

to incorporate - *incorporar, incorpore*

to jell or set, to curdle - *cuajar, cuaje*

to juice (as in lemons) - *exprimir, exprima*

to keep, preserve, maintain, or conserve - *conservar, conserve*

to knead - *amasar, amase*

to lard, usually to wrap meat or poultry in bacon - *mechar, meche*

to leave - *dejar, deje*

to leave to cool, let it cool - *dejar enfriar*

to leave to reduce, let it reduce - *dejar reducir*

to let stand, to allow to rest, to steep - *reposar, repose*

to like - *gustar, guste*

to line or cover (as in a baking pan) - *forrar, forre*

to liquify - *liquidar, liquide*

to blend or liquify (as in a blender) - *licuar, licue*

to lower, to go down - *bajar, baje*

to make holes in the bottom - *pinchar el fondo*

to make holes in, to perforate - *agujerear, agujeree*

to make some slices or splits in it - *hágale unas rajaduras*

to marinade or pickle - *escabechar, escabeche*

to marinate - *marinar, marine*

to marinate and mash - *macerar, macere*

to marinate, season, or rub meat - *adobar, adobe*

to mark - *marcar, marque*

to mash - *majar, maje*

to measure - *medir, mida*

to melt - *derretir, derrita*

to melt - *fundir, funda*

to mix, blend, or emulsify - *mezclar, mezcle*

to moisten - *humedecer, humedezca*

to mold, or to put into a mold - *moldear, moldee*

to obtain or acquire - *adquirir, adquiera*
to oil or grease - *aceitar, aceite*
to order the food - *ordenar la comida*
to parch, scorch, or overcook purposely - *requemar, requeme*
to pass through - *pasar, pase*
to peel - *pelar, pele*
to place or put - *poner, ponga*
to poach - *escalfar, escalfe* or *pochar, poche*
to pour or spill - *verter, vierta*
to prefer - *preferir, prefiera*
to prepare - *preparar, prepare*
to puncture or prick - *pinchar, pinche*
to put aside, reserve - *reservar, reserve*
to put together, to prepare - *confeccionar, confeccione*
to raise or lift - *levantar, levante*
to reduce - *reducir, reduzca*
to re-fry - *refreír, refría*
to reheat - *recalentar, recaliente*
to release or give off - *desprender, desprenda*
to remove or take away - *quitar, quite*
to remove or take away - *retirar, retire*
to return, to revert - *volver, vuelva*
to rinse - *enjuagar, enjuague*
to rip or tear - *rasgar, rasgue*
to roast - *asar, ase*
to roll in breadcrumbs - *empanar, empane*
to roll in flour - *enharinar, enharine*
to roll out with the rolling pin - *estirar con el rodillo*
to roll up - *enrollar, enrolle*
to rub - *frotar, frote*
to run under water - *correr bajo el agua, pasar bajo el agua*
to salt or make salty - *salar, sale*
to sauté - *saltear, saltee*
to sauté, to fry lightly - *sofreír, sofría*
to savor, to taste - *saborear, saboree*

to scatter or spread - *esparcir, esparza*

to scrape - *raspar, raspe*

to seal - *sellar, selle*

to sear - *sellar, selle*

to season - *sazonar, sazone*

to season (with salt & pepper) - *salpimentar, salpimiente*

to secure, to fasten - *asegurar, asegure*

to serve - *servir, sirva*

to shake - *menear, menee*

to shake - *sacudir, sacuda*

to share - *compartir, comparta*

to shred - *deshebrar, deshebre*

to sieve or sift - *tamizar, tamice*

to sift - *cerner, cierna*

to simmer (literally "cook over a low flame") - *cocer a fuego lento*

to singe or scorch - *chamuscar, chamusque*

to slice - *rebanar, rebane*

to soak - *remojar, remoje*

to soften or make tender - *enternecer, enternezca*

to soften or smoothe - *suavizar, suavice*

to soften, to tenderize - *ablandar, ablande*

to split, break, or cut - *partir, parta*

to spray, to sprinkle - *rociar, rocíe*

to spread out - *extender, extienda*

to sprinkle - *espolvorear, espolvoree*

to sprinkle, splash, or spray, as with water or another liquid - *salpicar, salpique*

to squeeze - *exprimir, exprima*

to steam - *cocer al vapor*

to stew - *guisar, guise*

to stir - *revolver, revuelva*

to stir, or to remove - *remover, remueva*

to strain or filter - *colar, cuele*

to stretch or extend - *estirar, estire*

to stuff, to fill, to refill - *rellenar, rellene*

to sweat, as in to sweat an onion - *sudar, sude*
to take out, to take off, to remove - *sacar, saque*
to take, to drink - *tomar, tome*
to taste, or as you like - *al gusto*
to tear in pieces or to chop - *retazar, retace*
to tear or shred into pieces - *despedazar, despedace*
to thicken - *adquirir cuerpo*
to thicken or coagulate - *espesar, espese*
to throw away - *tirar, tire*
to throw into the trash, to throw away - *tirar a la basura*
to try or to taste, to proof or to test - *probar, pruebe*
to turn over - *girar, gire*
to uncover, remove the lid - *destapar, destape*
to unmold - *desmoldear, desmoldee*
to wait (for) - *esperar, espere*
to warm or heat up - *calentar, caliente*
to warm up - *entibiar, entibie*
to wash or scrub - *fregar, friegue*
to wet - *mojar, móje*
to work (as in work the dough), to beat until smooth - *trabajar, trabaje*
to work the flour - *trabajar la harina*
to wrap or wrap up - *envolver, envuelva*
to your liking - *de su agrado*
toasted - *tostado/a*
together - *juntos*
tomato sauce mixed with cream, or ketchup mixed with mayonnaise - *salsa rosada*
too little of, lack of - *le falta*
too much of, surplus of - *le sobra*
too salty - *demasiado salado*
too sweet - *demasiado dulce*
tube - *tubo*
turn off the heat - *apague el fuego*
underdone - *no suficiente*
unseasoned - *no sazonado/a*

until - *hasta que*
until it boils - *hasta que hierva*
until you get, achieve, or obtain - *hasta conseguir...*
variety - *variedad*
vegan - *vegano/a*
vegetarian - *vegetariano/a*
vinegary - *avinagrado/a, vinagroso*
vitamins - *vitaminas*
wait until... - *espere hasta que...*
waiter, waitress - *camarero, camarera*
warm, temperate - *templado/a*
well browned - *bien dorado/a*
well cooked - *bien cocido/a*
well done (as in meat) - *bien cocido/a or bien hecho*
well heated - *bien caliente*
wet - *mojado/a*
when it boils - *a punto de hervir*
when it froths or forms stiff peaks - *a punto de nieve*
when it thickens - *a punto de espesor*
with alcohol, alcoholic - *con alcohol*
with bone - *con hueso*
with skin - *con piel*
with...on top - *con...encima*
without artificial flavorings - *sin saborizantes artificiales*
without bone, boneless - *sin hueso*
without letting (it) brown - *sin dejar dorar*
without skin, skinless - *sin piel*
without the crust or rind - *sin la costra*

Glosario de Términos de Cocina y Adjetivos Útiles - Glossary of Cooking Terms and Helpful Adjectives (*Spanish* to English)

¡Buen Provecho! - Enjoy your meal!

¡Salud! - Cheers! To your health!

¿Tiene hambre? - Are you hungry?

a fuego alto - on a high heat

a fuego lento, a fuego bajo - on a low heat

a fuego medio, a fuego moderado - on a medium heat

a la barbacoa - barbecued

a la leña - grilled or roasted over a wood fire

a la mitad - in half

a la parrilla - grilled on an open grate

a la plancha - grilled on a grill pan, broiled

a las brasas - charcoal grilled

a punto de espesor - when it thickens

a punto de hervir - when it boils

a punto de nieve - when it froths or forms stiff peaks

a punto de... - on the point of... (when)

ablandar, ablande - to soften, to tenderize

abombar, abombe - to curve or hollow out

acanalado/a - grooved, corrugated

aceitar, aceite - to oil or grease

ácido/a - acidic, sour

acompañados/as - accompanied

acompañar, acompañe - to accompany, to go well with

aderezar, aderece - to dress or season

aderezo - dressing, seasoning
adición - addition
adicionar, adicione - to add or to augment
adobado/a - marinated
adobar, adobe - to marinate, season, or rub meat
adobo - seasoning rub for meat
adquirir cuerpo - to thicken
adquirir, adquiera - to obtain or acquire
afrutado/a - fruity
agradable - enjoyable, nice
agregar, agregue - to add
agridulce - bittersweet, sweet & sour
agrio/a - sour
agua hirviendo - boiling water
agujerear, agujeree - to make holes in, to perforate
ahumado/a - smoked, smokey
al ajillo - fried or sauted with garlic
al carbón - charcoal grilled
al gusto - to taste, or as you like
al horno - baked or roasted in the oven
al término de su gusto - finished to your liking (your taste)
al vapor - steamed
albondigas - meatballs
alcohólico, con alcohol - alcoholic
alergia alimentaria - food allergy
algunos/as - some
alimentación - nutrition, nourishment
almorzar, almuerce - to have lunch
almuerzo - lunch
alrededor - around
alternando/a - alternating
alternar, alterne - to alternate
amargo/a - bitter, unsweetened
amasar, amase - to knead
añadir, añada - to add

apague el fuego - turn off the heat

aparte - separately

aproximadamente - approximately

asado/a - roasted

asar, ase - to roast

asegurar, asegure - to secure, to fasten

asegure con palillos de madera - secure with wooden toothpicks

avanzado/a - advanced

avinagrado/a - vinegary

bajar, baje - to lower, to go down

baje el fuego - lower the heat

baje la intensidad del fuego - lower the intensity of the heat

bajo/a en grasa - low-fat

balanza - scales for weighing

bañar, bañe - to coat, dip or bathe

barnizar, barnice - to coat or glaze (literally "to varnish")

barra de... - stick of (butter, margarine)

bastante - quite, enough

bata los huevos - beat the eggs

batido para rebozar - batter

batido/a - beaten, whipped

batir, bata - to blend, beat, whip, or whisk

beber, beba - to drink

bebidas - beverages

bien aromático/a - fragrant

bien caliente - well heated

bien cocido/a - well cooked, well done (as in meat)

bien dorado/a - well browned

bien hecho - well-done (meat)

blando/a - soft, pliant

blanquear, blanquee - to blanche, to whiten

bocadito or bocadillo - appetizer or snack

bola - ball

bolita - small ball

bolitas de carne - small meatballs

bollos - rolls, buns
brevemente - briefly
brocheta - brochette
bueno/a - good
bulbo - bulb
burbujas - bubbles
cabeza de ajo - head of garlic
caja - box or package
calcular, calcule - to calculate
caldo - broth
calentar, caliente - to warm or heat up
caliente - hot
camarero, camarera - waiter, waitress
cantidad - quantity, amount
capa - layer
caramelizado/a - caramelized
carbohidrato - carbohydrate
carne - meat
carnicería - butcher shop, meat market
carnicero - butcher
cascar, casque - to crack, chip, or break
cáscara - shell, husk or rind
casero/a - homemade
cda. (cucharada) - tablespoon
cdita. (cucharadita) - teaspoon
cebollas caramelizadas - caramelized onions
cena - dinner
cenar, cene - to dine, to eat dinner/supper
cerner, cierna - to sift
cernido/a - sifted
cerrar, cierre - to close or fasten
chamuscado/a - scorched, singed
chamuscar, chamusque - to singe or scorch
cocer a fuego lento - to simmer (literally "cook over a low flame")
cocer al vapor - to steam

cocer, cueza - to cook, to bake

cocido/a - cooked

cocinar, cocine - to cook

colar, cuele - to strain or filter

colesterol - cholesterol

colocar, coloque - to arrange, to place

comer, coma - to eat

comida - food or meal

comida basura - junk food

comida rápida - fast food

compartir, comparta - to share

con alcohol - with alcohol, alcoholic

con cuidado - gently (literally "with care")

con hueso - with bone

con piel - with skin

con...encima - with...on top

condensado/a - condensed

condimentar, condimente - to dress or season

confeccionar, confeccione - to put together, to prepare

congelado/a - frozen

congelar, congele - to freeze

conservar, conserve - to keep, preserve, maintain, or conserve

consistencia - consistency

corona de... - crown of...

correr bajo el agua - to run under water

cortado/a - cut or chopped

cortado/a por la mitad - cut in half

cortar en aros - to cut into rings

cortar en cuartos - to cut into quarters

cortar en cubos - to cut into cubes, to dice

cortar en dos - to cut in two

cortar en longas - to cut into long slices

cortar en palitos - to cut into sticks

cortar in rodajas - to cut into small discs

cortar, corte - to cut or chop

corte una tapita - to cut off the top or cap

crema - cream

cremoso/a - creamy

crepas - crepes

cristalizado/a - crystalized

cristalizar, cristalice - to crystallize

crudo/a - raw, undercooked

crujiente - crunchy, crispy

cuadrados - squares

cuajar, cuaje - to jell or set, to curdle

cubierto - covered

cubitos de... - cubes or dice of...

cubrir, cubra - to cover

cucharadas colmadas, cucharadas coperas - heaping tablespoons

cuerpo - body

cuidadosamente - carefully

corrugado/a - grooved, corrugated

dados de... - cubes or dice of...

dándole - giving it...

de su agrado - to your liking

deber, deba - must, should, ought to

decorar, decore - to decorate

dejar enfriar - to leave to cool, let it cool

dejar reducir - to leave to reduce, let it reduce

dejar, deje - to leave

delgado/a - thin

delicioso/a - delicious

demasiado dulce - too sweet

demasiado salado - too salty

denso/a - dense

derretido/a - melted

derretir, derrita - to melt

desayunar, desayune - to eat breakfast

desayuno - breakfast

descongelado/a - defrosted

descongelar, descongele - to defrost, to thaw

descremado/a - non-fat, skimmed, as in milk

deseado/a - desired

desgrasado/a - defatted, skim

deshebrar, deshebre - to shred

deshidratado/a - dehydrated

deshidratar, deshidrate - to dehydrate

deshuesado/a - deboned

deslactosado/a - lactose-free

desleír, deslía - to dissolve or thin in liquid (not commonly used)

desmenuzado/a - crumbled or shredded

desmenuzar, desmenuce - to crumble or to flake

desmoldear, desmoldee - to unmold

despedazar, despedace - to tear or shred into pieces

desprender, desprenda - to release or give off

destapar, destape - to uncover, remove the lid

dientes de ajo - cloves of garlic

dieta saludable - healthy diet

difícil - difficult

diluir, diluya - to dilute

disfrutar, disfrute - to enjoy

disolver, disuelva - to dissolve

disponer, disponga - to arrange or line up

disuelto/a - dissolved

dividir, divida - to divide

doblar, doble - to double or to fold over

dorado/a - browned

dorar, dore - to brown

dore por ambos lados - brown on both sides

dulce - sweet

duro/a - hard, tough

echado a perder - spoiled

el lado de la piel - skin-side

empanada - pie, turnover

empanar, empane - to roll in breadcrumbs

empanizado/a - breaded
empanizar, empanice - to bread something
en churrasco - charbroiled
en cubos - cut into cubes
en juliana - julienned, cut into thin strips
en parilla - grilled
en pedacitos - flaked
en polvo - powdered
encima - atop, on top of
encurtido/a - pickled
endurecer, endurezca - to harden
enfriar, enfrie - to chill or cool
engrasado/a - greased
engrasar, engrase - to grease or oil
engrase y enharine - grease and flour (a pan)
enharinar, enharine - to roll in flour
enjuagar, enjuague - to rinse
enlatado/a - canned
enrollar, enrolle - to roll up
ensalada - salad
enternecer, enternezca - to soften or make tender
entero/a - entire or whole
entibiar, entibie - to warm up
entretanto - meanwhile, in the meantime
envolver, envuelva - to wrap or wrap up
escabechar, escabeche - to marinade or pickle
escabeche - a marinade, pickle, or brine
escalfado/a - poached
escalfar, escalfe - to poach
escurrido/a - drained
escurrir, escurra - to drain
espalda - back
espalda con espalda - back to back
esparcir, esparza - to scatter or spread
esperar, espere - to wait (for)

espere hasta que... - wait until...

espesar, espese - to thicken or coagulate

espolvorear, espolvoree - to sprinkle

espuma - foam

espumar, espume - to froth or foam, to skim off

espumoso/a - frothy, bubbly

estirar con el rodillo - to roll out with the rolling pin

estirar, estire - to stretch or extend

estofado/a - stewed

evaporado/a - evaporated

excelente - excellent

exprimido/a - squeezed

exprimir, exprima - to squeeze, to juice (as in lemons)

extender, extienda - to spread out

extraer, extraiga - to extract or pull out

fácil - easy

fibroso - stringy

filete de... - fillet of...

finamente cortado/a - finely chopped

fino/a - thin, fine

fondo - bottom, base

formar un disco - to form a disc

formar una bola - to form a ball

formar, forme - to form or shape

forrar, forre - to line or cover (as in a baking pan)

fregar, friegue - to wash or scrub

freír, fría - to fry

fresco/a - fresh, cool

frío/a - cold

frito/a - fried

frotar, frote - to rub

frozen food - alimentos congelados

fuego - fire or heat

fuerte - strong

fundido/a - melted, molten

fundiendo - melting
fundir, funda - to melt
g. (gramo) - gram
gaseoso/a - fizzy
generoso/a - full, generous
gentilmente - gently
girar, gire - to turn over
glaseado/a, con glasé - glazed
gotas - drops
gotitas - droplets
gramo (g.) - gram
grande - large
granos - grains or beans, as in coffee beans
grasa - grease or fat
grasiento - greasy
gratinado/a - cooked au gratin
gratinar, gratine - to cook au gratin (usually covered in breadcrumbs
    and cheese and baked or browned in the oven)
grosor - thickness
gruesamente - thickly
grueso/a - thick
guisado/a - stewed
guisar, guise - to stew
gustar, guste - to like
hacer, haga - to do or to make
hágale unas rajaduras - to make some slices or splits in it
harina cernida - sifted flour
hasta conseguir... - until you get, achieve, or obtain
hasta que - until
hasta que hierva - until it boils
hender, hienda - to cleave, slit, crack
hervido/a - boiled
hervir, hierva - to boil
hidratado/a - rehydrated
hidratar, hidrate - to hydrate

hielo - ice
hielo en cubitos - ice cubes
hierbas - herbs
hirviendo/a - boiling
hoja - leaf or sheet
hojitas - small leaves
homogénea - homogenous
hora - hour
horneado/a - baked
hornear, hornee - to bake
horno - oven
hueco - hole
huequitos - small holes
huesos - bones
huevo blando - soft-boiled egg
huevo duro - hard-boiled egg
humedecer, humedezca - to moisten
incorporar, incorpore - to incorporate
ingredientes - ingredients
intermedio/a - intermediate
jugoso/a - juicy
juliana - julienne
juntos - together
kilogramo (kilo, kg.) - kilogram
laminas - sheets
lamprear, lampree - to cook or season with wine
lata de... - can of...
le falta - too little of, lack of
le sobra - too much of, surplus of
levantar, levante - to raise or lift
levemente aceitado/a - lightly oiled
licuado/a - liquified, blended
licuar, licue - to blend or liquify (as in a blender)
ligeramente - slightly
ligeramente tostado/a - slightly toasted

ligero/a - light
limpiar, limpie - to clean
liquidar, liquide - to liquify
liquido/a - liquid
liso/a - smooth
listo/a - ready
llevar a ebullición - to bring to the boil
llevar, lleve - to carry or take
macerar, macere - to marinate and mash
machacado/a - crushed
machacar, machaque - to crush
maduro/a - ripe, mature
majado/a - mashed
majar, maje - to mash
malo/a - bad
manojo - handful or bunch
mantequilla derretida - melted butter
marcar, marque - to mark
marinado/a - marinated
marinar, marine - to marinate
marque en la parilla - to give something grill marks
mas grande - larger
mas pequeño/a - smaller
masa - dough
mechar, meche - to lard, usually to wrap meat or poultry in bacon
medallones de... - medallions of...
mediano/a - medium
medida - measurement
medio/a - half
medio-bajo - medium low (as in heat)
medir, mida - to measure
menear, menee - to shake
menú - menu
menú del dia - menu of the day
merengue - meringue

mermelada - marmalade or jam

mezcla - mixture

mezclado/a - blended

mezclar, mezcle - to mix, blend, or emulsify

minutos - minutes

mitad - half

mojado/a - wet

mojar, móje - to wet

moldear, moldee - to mold, or to put into a mold

moler, muela - to grind or mill

molido/a - ground

nevar las claras - froth the egg whites to peaks (literally "to snow the clear")

nivel de complejidad - level of complexity

nivel de dificultad - level of difficulty

no sazonado/a - unseasoned

no seco - not dry

no suficiente - not sufficient, underdone

numero de porciones - number of portions

nutrientes - nutrients

ordenar la comida - to order the food

organico/a - organic

orilla - edge or border

palitos - sticks, stalks, or stems

palitos de pan - breadsticks

palitos de queso - cheese sticks

pan rallado - bread crumbs

panadería - bakery

papa al horno - baked potato

papas fritas - french fries

paquete - packet or package

para 10 personas - serves 10 persons

parrilla - barbecue grate

partido/a - divided

partir, parta - to split, break, or cut

pasado/a - stale (bread) or bad (meat)

pasar por harina - to dredge in flour

pasar, pase - to pass through

pasar bajo el agua - to run under water

pastel - pastry or pie

pastel de queso - cheesecake

pastelería - pastry shop

pedacito - small piece or slice

pedazo - piece or slice

pedir, pida - to ask for, to order

pelar, pele - to peel, peel

pequeño/a - small

pesado/a - heavy, weighty

peso escurrido - drained weight

picadillo - hash

picado/a - chopped, minced

picado/a en trozos finos - chopped in small pieces

picado/a fino or finamente picado/a - finely chopped

picante - spicy, tangy

picar, pique - to finely chop or mince

piezas - pieces

pimienta negra molida fresca - black pepper freshly ground

pinchar el fondo - to make holes in the bottom

pinchar, pinche - to puncture or prick

pizca - dash or pinch (of seasoning)

plato (de una comida) - course, dish

plegar, pliegue - to fold

pochado/a - poached

pochar, poche - to poach

poco a poco - little by little

poco hecho, or poco asado - rare (meat)

poner, ponga - to place or put

por ambos lados - on both sides

por la mitad - in half

por ultimo - lastly

por un par de minutos - for a couple of minutes

porción - portion

postre - dessert

precalentado/a - preheated

precalentar, precaliente - to preheat

preferir, prefiera - to prefer

preparación - preparation

preparado/a - prepared

preparar, prepare - to prepare

probar, pruebe - to try or to taste, to proof or to test

proteina - protein

pruebe la sazón - taste to check the seasoning

pulgadas - inches

puré - purée

puré de papas - mashed potatoes

quemado/a - burnt

queque - cake

queso fundido - melted (molten) cheese

quitar, quite - to remove or take away

racimo de uvas - bunch or cluster of grapes

rajadura - a crack or split

rallado/a - grated

ralladura - grated peel or rind

ralladura de limón - lemon zest

rallar, ralle - to grate

ralo/a - thin

ramita - sprig, as in sprig of rosemary

rasgar, rasgue - to rip or tear

raspar, raspe - to scrape

rebanado/a - sliced

rebanar, rebane - to slice

rebozar, reboce - to dip in batter or eggs

recalentar, recaliente - to reheat

receta - recipe

recién exprimido - freshly squeezed

rectificar, rectifique - to correct, to rectify
reducción - reduction
reducir, reduzca - to reduce
refractario - heat-resistant, oven-proof
refreír, refría - to re-fry
rellenar, rellene - to stuff, to fill, to refill
relleno/a - stuffed, filled, or stuffing
remojar, remoje - to soak
remover, remueva - to stir, or to remove
repartir, reparta - to divide, to apportion, to distribute
reposar, repose - to let stand, to allow to rest, to steep
requemar, requeme - to parch, scorch, or overcook purposely
reservar, reserve - to put aside, reserve
retazar, retace - to tear in pieces or to chop
retirar, retire - to remove or take away
retire del fuego - take off the heat
retire del horno - take out of the oven
reventar, reviente - to burst or crack open
revolver, revuelva - to stir
revolver constantemente - stir constantly
revolviendo siempre - stirring continually
revuelto/a - scrambled, turned over
rico/a - delicious (literally "rich")
riquísimo - luscious, delicious
rociar, rocíe - to spray, to sprinkle
rodaja - round slice
rollo - roll
rompa el hervor - bring to a boil
romper, rompa - to break or burst
sabor - taste or flavor
saborear, saboree - to savor, to taste
sabores - flavors
sabroso/a - tasty, flavorful
sacar de refrigeración - take out of the refrigerator
sacar del fuego - remove from the fire (take off the heat)

sacar, saque - to take out, to take off, to remove

sacudir, sacuda - to shake

salado/a - salty, salted, savory

salar, sale - to salt or make salty

salpicar, salpique - to sprinkle, splash, or spray, as with water or another liquid

salpimentar, salpimiente - to season (with salt & pepper)

salpimiente al gusto, sal y pimienta al gusto - salt and pepper to taste

salsa - sauce, salsa

salsa rosada - tomato sauce mixed with cream, or ketchup mixed with mayonnaise

salteado/a - sautéed

saltear, saltee - to sauté

sancochar, sancoche - to parboil

sándwich - sandwich

sazón - seasoning or flavoring

sazonar, sazone - to season

se tiene que masticar mucho - chewy

secando/a - drying

secar, seque - to dry

seco/a - dried

seguir, siga - to continue

segundo plato - second course or main course

sellado/a - seared

sellar, selle - to seal, to sear

sellar ambos lados - sear both sides

semi-duro - semi-hard

semilla - seed

sencillo/a - plain

servir inmediatamente - serve immediately

servir, sirva - to serve

si lo desea - if you desire

siga cocinando - continue cooking

siguiente - following, next

sin alcohol - non-alcoholic

sin dejar dorar - without letting (it) brown
sin hueso - without bone, boneless
sin la costra - without the crust or rind
sin piel - without skin, skinless
sin sabor - bland, flavorless
sin saborizantes artificiales - without artificial flavorings
sin semilla - seedless
sitio frío - cool place
sobras - leftovers
sobre una cama de... - on a bed of...
sobres de... - envelopes of...
sofreír, sofría - to sauté, to fry lightly
sopa - soup
soso/a - bland, flavorless
suave - soft, mild
suavizar, suavice - to soften or smoothe
sudado/a - cooked in very little water (literally, "sweaty")
sudar, sude - to sweat, as in to sweat an onion
superficie - surface area
surtido/a - assorted, an assortment
tajada, taja - slice
tajadita - small slice
tallo - stalk, stem, or shoot
tamaño - size
tamizar, tamice - to sieve or sift
tapado/a - covered
tapar, tape - to cover, to put the lid on
temperatura - temperature
temperatura ambiente - room temperature
temperatura interna de... - internal temperature of...
templado/a - warm, temperate
tenderizado/a - tenderized, tender
término medio - medium rare, as in steak
tibio/a - lukewarm, tepid
tiempo - time

tiempo de preparación - preparation time

tiempo de reposo - time to settle or rest

tierno/a - tender

tirar a la basura - to throw into the trash, to throw away

tirar, tire - to throw away

tiras - strips or shreds

tomar, tome - to take, to drink

tostado/a - toasted

tostar, tuéste - to toast

trabajar la harina - to work the flour

trabajar, trabaje - to work (as in work the dough), to beat until smooth

tres cuartos - medium well done, as in steak

triturado/a - crushed, or ground

triturar, triture - to crush or grind

trocitos - small pieces, chunks

trozo - piece

tubo - tube

un cartón de - a carton of...

un paquete de... - a package of...

una botella de... - a bottle of...

una lata de... - a can of...

una vez - once

una vez cocinado/a - once cooked

unos minutos - a few (some) minutes

unos segundos - a few (some) seconds

unos/as - some

untar, unte - to grease with oil or butter, to spread or smear

vaciar, vacie - to empty, to hollow out, to drain

vacío/a - empty or hollow

variedad - variety

vegano/a - vegan

vegetariano/a - vegetarian

verter, vierta - to pour or spill

vinagroso - vinegary

viscoso/a - gooey, viscous

COOKING IN COSTA RICA

vitaminas - vitamins
volcar, vuelque - to dump or pour
volver, vuelva - to return, to revert

Recipe Substitutions

Dairy

Buttermilk Substitute

Buttermilk in Costa Rica is called *leche agria,* but it is not widely available in grocery stores. You can make your own buttermilk substitute by mixing 1 tablespoon of white vinegar or lemon juice and enough milk to equal 1 cup and letting it stand for 5 minutes.

Another option, which I often choose, is to substitute plain yogurt for buttermilk in recipes.

Half & Half

Half & half is generally not available in Costa Rica. To make your own, mix 1/4 cup *crema dulce* (heavy whipping cream) with 3/4 cup whole milk. If you are using lower fat milk (1% or 2%), adjust the proportions to 1/3 cup *crema dulce* and 2/3 cup low-fat milk. Shelf-stable *crema dulce* is widely available, but if you are lucky, you may be able to find fresh cream in the dairy case.

Another method of making half & half is to melt 4 teaspoons of unsalted butter and add enough whole milk to equal 1 cup.

Baking

Bread Flour

I have never seen bread flour in a grocery store in Costa Rica. Bread flour has a higher percentage of protein and gluten, which give a slightly higher rise and a bit more chew to baked goods. When a recipe calls for bread flour, you should still be able to get a good result by using all-purpose flour (*harina de trigo*).

Cake or Pastry Flour

Cake flour is another product I have never seen in Costa Rica. Like bread flour, the primary difference between it and all-purpose flour is the protein content. Where bread flour has a higher protein content, cake flour has a lower percentage of protein, which also reduces the gluten. To make homemade cake flour, just add cornstarch. For every cup of cake flour needed, place 2 tablespoons of cornstarch in a measuring cup, fill the rest with all-purpose flour, and mix well.

Self-Rising Flour

Self-rising flour is merely a mix of all-purpose flour, baking powder, and salt. For every 1 cup of all-purpose flour, add 1 1/2 teaspoons of baking powder and 1/2 teaspoon salt and whisk to mix thoroughly. For a bigger batch, just multiply the ingredients.

Homemade Bisquick©

While you may be able to find Bisquick© in higher end stores like Auto Mercado, it is expensive. I have never been able to find it closer to home. The solution, should you want to duplicate your favorite Bisquick©-based recipes in Costa Rica, is to make your own. While there are recipes to make larger quantities, since it has butter or shortening in it, I think it is better to make up just the quantity you need when you need it. This recipe, therefore, uses smaller quantities of everything and you can double or triple it as needed.

Ingredients:

- ◆ 1 cup all-purpose flour
- ◆ 1 1/2 teaspoons baking powder
- ◆ 1/4 tablespoon salt
- ◆ 1 tablespoon butter or shortening

Directions:

1. Sift flour, baking powder and salt and whisk together well.

2. Cut in butter with a pastry blender until mixture resembles fine crumbs. If you have a food processor, you can put the mixture in and pulse 4 or 5 times until it resembles fine crumbs.

3. If you are making a larger quantity, it is better to store the mixture in an airtight container in the refrigerator for up to 4 months.

Spice Mixes

Poultry Seasoning

The most important herb in poultry seasoning is sage. While I have never seen rubbed sage in Costa Rica, it is possible to find dried sage (*salvia*) in some of the larger markets like Mas x Menos and Auto Mercado. To round out the poultry seasoning, add a blend of the following, as available: thyme, marjoram, black pepper, and rosemary.

Ingredients:

For every teaspoon of poultry seasoning needed, substitute the following:

- 3/4 teaspoon sage
- 1/4 teaspoon blend of thyme, marjoram, black pepper, and/or rosemary
- Pinch of onion powder

Directions:

Blend all of the spices together and store in an air-tight container. You can also pulse them briefly in a spice grinder. Use for stuffing and poultry.

Chili Powder

Chili powder is one of those spice blends that I can find only rarely. It is helpful to have the option to make it at home from easier-to-find spices. I often run this through my spice grinder for a better mix.

Ingredients:

- 2 tablespoons paprika
- 2 teaspoons oregano
- 1 1/4 teaspoons cumin
- 1 1/4 teaspoons garlic powder
- 1 1/4 teaspoons cayenne pepper
- 3/4 teaspoon onion powder

Directions:

Mix everything together and use whenever a recipe calls for chili powder.

Apple Pie Spice

Apple pie spice is usually a mixture of ground cinnamon, nutmeg, and allspice. You can also add a dash of ground cloves or ginger, depending on your own taste preference.

Ingredients:

For every teaspoon of apple pie spice needed, substitute the following:
- 1/2 teaspoon ground cinnamon
- 1/4 teaspoon ground nutmeg
- 1/8 teaspoon ground allspice
- dash ground cloves or ginger (optional)

If you want to make a larger quantity to have some on hand, here are the proportions:
- 2 tablespoons ground cinnamon
- 1 teaspoon ground nutmeg
- 1/2 teaspoon ground allspice
- 1/8 teaspoon ground cloves or ginger (optional)

Directions:

Mix all the spices together, and store in an airtight container.

Pumpkin Pie Spice

Pumpkin pie spice is similar to apple pie spice. At its most basic, it is a combination of ground cinnamon, ginger, nutmeg, and allspice. The quantities below are suggestions; you can add more or less of anything to suit your own taste. You can also add ground cloves in the same quantity as the allspice or even a pinch of cardamom.

Ingredients:

For every teaspoon of pumpkin pie spice needed, substitute the following:
- 1/2 teaspoon ground cinnamon
- 1/4 teaspoon ground ginger
- 1/8 to 1/4 teaspoon ground allspice
- 1/8 teaspoon ground nutmeg

If you want to make a larger quantity to have some on hand, here are the proportions:
- 2 tablespoons ground cinnamon
- 1 teaspoon ground ginger
- 1/2 to 1 teaspoon ground allspice
- 1/2 to 1 teaspoon ground nutmeg

Directions:

Mix all the spices together, and store in an airtight container.

Pantry Staples

Canned Pumpkin Substitute

Now that you have the recipe for pumpkin pie spice, all you need is some canned pumpkin to make a pie or a loaf of pumpkin bread...or do you? Though it is a bit time-consuming, it's easy to make homemade pumpkin puree. All you need are some big chunks of the hard, orange *ayote* or *calabaza* squash and an oven. Here's how you do it.

Directions:

1. Remove the seeds and fibrous pulp from the center of the squash. (If you like, you can separate out the seeds, sprinkle them with some garlic powder, cumin, and/or other spices, and roast them to make crunchy pumpkin seeds for snacks or to sprinkle on salads.)
2. Arrange the squash pieces on a baking sheet, cover with foil, and roast at 350 degrees for about an hour until tender.
3. Remove the skins from the flesh and discard.
4. Puree the roasted flesh in a food processor or mash with a potato masher.

Notes:

I usually make a big batch of puree and freeze in pint-sized zip-lock bags in 2 cup portions. Then, when I get the urge to bake pumpkin bread or pie, I just take a bag out of the freezer. You can also use the puree for soups.

Cream of Anything Soup Substitute

Sure, opening a can of cream of mushroom, cream of celery, or cream of asparagus soup is easy, but it also has many undesirable ingredients. Plus, if you can find it in Costa Rica, it's going to be about three times the price you would pay back home. This recipe is an easy substitute. You can make the following base, then add sautéed mushrooms, celery, asparagus, bits of cooked chicken, or whatever else you want, then use it in any recipes that call for a can of "cream of something" soup. I often use it as a sauce with cooked pasta, steamed carrots, broccoli, and chayote, and chunks of chicken.

Ingredients to equal one can of prepared cream soup:

* 2 tablespoons butter
* 3 tablespoons all-purpose flour
* 1/2 cup low sodium chicken broth
* 1/2 cup milk (whole or low-fat)
* salt and pepper

Directions:

1. Start by making a roux: melt butter in a saucepan over low heat, then stir in the flour, whisking constantly until smooth.

2. Slowly add the chicken broth and milk while you continue whisking until the mixture is thick and smooth.

3. Add salt and pepper to taste.

Broth Substitute

While there is nothing like homemade broth, in a pinch you can add one bouillon cube to a cup of boiling water and stir. Knorr and Maggi are common brands in Costa Rica. One thing to note about bouillon cubes is that they do contain MSG and lots of sodium, so I use them sparingly.

For another option, see the recipe for "Vegetable Bouillon Paste" in the section "Bonus Recipes from Costa Rica Bloggers and Cooks."

Tahini

Tahini is expensive to buy but inexpensive and easy to make. You can find *semillas ajonjoli* (sesame seeds) just about everywhere. Buy some and roast in a dry pan until golden brown and fragrant. Then, all you need to do is grind them into a paste using a spice grinder or the small bowl of a food processor. Store the tahini in a glass jar in your fridge and it will keep for months.

Gloria's Recipes

Breakfast Sausage

Breakfast sausage was one of those things I could never find in Costa Rica and missed until I found out how easy it is to replicate. It all starts with ground pork. You can find pork already ground in many *carnicerías* (butcher shops) but I prefer to have it freshly ground. Many *carnicerías* will be able to grind it while you wait. I usually ask for *posta de cerdo,* which has some fat on it. You can make your sausage hotter by adding 1/2 teaspoon of cayenne pepper to the spice blend.

Ingredients:

- 16 ounces (1/2 kilo) ground pork
- 1 teaspoon salt
- 1/2 teaspoon dried parsley
- 1/4 teaspoon sage (or more to taste)
- 1/4 teaspoon fresh coarse ground black pepper
- 1/4 teaspoon dried thyme
- 1/4 teaspoon crushed red pepper flakes (optional)
- 1/4 teaspoon coriander (optional)

Directions:

1. Measure and mix the spice blend.

2. Add to the ground pork and mix well.

3. Form into patties and pan fry, or freeze for later.

Italian Sausage

With my Italian heritage, Italian sausage with peppers and onions was a regular feature of celebrations throughout my life. Whether it was 4th of July or New Year's Eve, sausage and peppers would show up on the menu. But in Costa Rica, at least in our town, it was impossible to find an authentic tasting version so I started making my own.

The key ingredient in Italian sausage is fennel seed, which is difficult to find in Costa Rica, so if you want to try this recipe, you will need to pack a jar of fennel seed in your luggage or have a visiting friend bring you some. If you are in the Escazú area of Costa Rica, you may find it at the specialty store *Cúrcuma* (see resource section for details). Grind the whole fennel seeds in your spice grinder or do it manually in a mortar and pestle.

As with the breakfast sausage recipe, I usually use *posta de cerdo,* which has some fat on it, and have the pork freshly ground at the *carnicería.* I do not stuff my sausage meat into casings, though you could most likely buy casings at a *carnicería.* Instead, I prepare it loose to use in homemade tomato sauce, form it into patties to serve on a roll with sausage and peppers, or roll it into tiny meatballs to add to soup.

Ingredients:

- 1 kg. ground pork
- 1 tablespoon salt
- 2 teaspoons fennel seed, ground
- 1 tablespoon finely minced fresh garlic
- 1 teaspoon ground black pepper
- 1 teaspoon crushed red pepper
- 3 tablespoons red wine vinegar

Directions:

Mix all the ingredients together. You can use it immediately or put it in the refrigerator for about 12 hours to allow time for the flavors to develop.

Chipotle Beef Chili

This quick and easy chili gets its smoky flavor from chipotle chili powder (which is getting easier to find in Costa Rica). If you can't find chipotle powder, you can substitute one or two canned chipotle chilies which are readily available.

Ingredients:

- 1 lb. (or 1/2 kilo) ground beef
- 1 tablespoon olive oil
- 1 large yellow onion, chopped
- 4 garlic cloves, chopped
- 2-3 teaspoons chipotle chili powder
- 2 teaspoons dried oregano
- 2 teaspoons ground cumin
- 1 pouch (4 oz) tomato paste, such as *Natura's Pasta de Tomate*
- 1/2 canned jalapeño, chopped
- 2 cans red beans or 4 cups cooked dried red beans
- 2 cans black beans or 4 cups cooked dried black beans
- 2 cups chicken broth, or 2 chicken bouillon cubes and 2 cups water
- 1 can diced tomatoes or 2 cups diced fresh tomatoes
- Salt and pepper to taste

Toppings (optional)

- sour cream (natilla)
- shredded cheddar cheese
- sliced green onions
- chopped avocado

Directions:

1. Brown the ground beef in the olive oil in a Dutch oven or heavy-bottomed pot and transfer to a plate.

2. Add the onion and sauté several minutes until tender.

3. Add the garlic, chipotle chili powder, oregano, and cumin and cook for a couple of minutes until the garlic is fragrant.

4. Stir in the tomato paste and continue to cook another couple of minutes.

5. Add the jalapeño, red and black beans, chicken broth, tomatoes, and browned ground beef.

6. Bring to a boil and simmer 30 minutes or more.

7. Adjust seasonings with salt and pepper to taste, if needed.

8. Serve with toppings of choice and tortilla chips.

Paul's Favorite Coleslaw

This coleslaw recipe is similar to the KFC version. It is reminiscent of the coleslaw my husband, Paul's, mother made when he was growing up and it's his favorite. I use my food processor to shred the cabbage and carrot but you can also do it by hand with a knife or mandolin.

Buttermilk is not commonly available in Costa Rica. You can make a substitute with a bit of vinegar or lemon juice in regular milk, or just use yogurt instead (see "Recipe Substitutions" section for buttermilk substitute recipe).

Ingredients:

- 1 medium head of green cabbage
- 1 medium carrot
- 1/4 cup sugar
- 1/2 teaspoon salt
- 1/8 teaspoon pepper
- 1/4 cup milk
- 1/2 cup mayonnaise
- 1/4 cup plain yogurt or buttermilk
- 3 tablespoons apple cider vinegar
- 2 1/2 tablespoons lemon juice (I use *limón mandarino)*

Directions:

1. Shred or finely chop the cabbage and carrot and place in a large mixing bowl.

2. Make dressing by combining all of the other ingredients and mix until smooth.

3. Add dressing to shredded vegetables and mix well.

4. Refrigerate.

Hummus Four Ways

Hummus is one of those items we bought regularly at Trader Joe's. It is easy to make if you have a food processor and lends itself to many different variations. Following is the basic recipe plus three ways to spice it up. I usually make a double batch since it keeps well in the refrigerator for at least a week.

Basic Hummus Recipe

Ingredients:

- 1 can chickpeas (garbanzo beans), drained
- 2 cloves garlic
- 1 teaspoon ground cumin
- 1 lemon or lime, juiced (I use *limón mandarino*)
- 1/4 teaspoon sea salt, or more to taste
- 1-2 tablespoons extra virgin olive oil
- 1 tablespoon tahini (optional)

Directions:

1. Put the garlic cloves in the bowl of a food processor with the S blade and finely mince.

2. Add the chickpeas, cumin, lime juice, salt, and tahini (if you are using it.)

3. Slowly add the olive oil through the top chute while you process the ingredients on high speed until the mixture becomes a smooth paste.

4. I sometimes top the hummus with extra virgin olive oil and a grinding of pepper.

5. Serve with crackers, tortilla chips, sliced rounds of carrot or cucumber, or the more traditional pita wedges if you can find them or want to bake them.

Variations:

Spicy Hummus

Add 1/2 teaspoon crushed red pepper flakes to the other ingredients and process until smooth.

Smoky Chipotle Hummus

Add 1 canned chipotle chili in adobo sauce or 1 teaspoon ground chipotle chili powder to the other ingredients and process until smooth.

Roasted Garlic Hummus

To roast garlic in the oven: Slice the top off a head of garlic and drizzle with olive oil. Wrap the garlic in aluminum foil and roast in the oven at 350°F for about 40 minutes, until tender. Let it cool for about 10 minutes, and then squeeze the roasted garlic out of the skin. Add to the other ingredients and process until smooth.

Gloria's Pumpkin Bread

This is a delicious, moist, pumpkin bread, without all the oil in traditional recipes. I make it often during the holidays to give as gifts. For our Tico friends, especially, it is a welcome and unusual treat. And for our friends from the States, it is a taste of home. If you have prepared pumpkin pie spice, you can substitute 4 1/2 teaspoons of that for the cinnamon, nutmeg, and allspice called for in the recipe. Topping the loaves with chopped nuts gives a bit of crunch. The raisins give a bit of extra sweetness.

Yield: 2 loaves; 12 slices per loaf

Ingredients:

- 2 cups all-purpose flour
- 1 1/3 cup whole wheat flour
- 1 tablespoon baking powder
- 2 teaspoons baking soda
- 1 teaspoon salt
- 2 1/2 teaspoons ground cinnamon
- 1 1/2 teaspoons ground nutmeg
- 1/2 teaspoon ground allspice
- 2 cups granulated sugar
- 4 large eggs
- 1/2 cup canola oil
- 1/2 cup plain yogurt or buttermilk
- 2/3 cup water
- 1 (15-ounce) can pumpkin or 2 cups homemade pumpkin puree
- 3/4 cup raisins (optional)
- Cooking spray
- 1/3 cup chopped pecans or walnuts (optional)

Directions:

1. Preheat oven to 350°F.

2. Lightly spoon the flours into dry measuring cups; level with a knife. Combine flours and next 6 ingredients (through allspice) in a bowl and set aside.

3. Place sugar, eggs, oil, and buttermilk or yogurt in a large bowl; beat with a mixer at high speed until well blended.

4. Add 2/3 cup water and pumpkin, beating at low speed until blended.

5. Add flour mixture to pumpkin mixture, beating at low speed just until combined.

6. Add raisins, if desired.

7. Spoon batter into 2 loaf pans coated with cooking spray. Sprinkle nuts (optional) evenly over batter.

8. Bake at 350°F for 1 hour or until a wooden toothpick inserted in center comes out clean. Cool 10 minutes in pans on a wire rack; remove from pans. Cool completely on wire rack.

Carrot Cake with Tropical Cream Cheese Frosting

I wanted a healthier and lower fat carrot cake recipe that I could make here in Costa Rica, so I started with a Cooking Light recipe and adapted it for use with local ingredients. I've also included the Spanish names of all the ingredients.

Serves 8

Ingredients:

Cake:
- 1 cup all-purpose flour *(harina de trigo)*
- 3/4 cup whole wheat flour *(harina integral)*
- 3/4 cup quick-cooking oats *(avena "rapido" or "al minuto")*
- 2 teaspoons ground cinnamon *(canela)*
- 1 1/2 teaspoons baking powder *(polvo para hornear)*
- 1/2 teaspoon baking soda *(bicarbonato de sodio)*
- 1/4 teaspoon salt *(sal)*
- 3/4 cup packed brown sugar *(azúcar moreno or tapa de dulce molida)*
- 2 tablespoons butter, softened *(mantequilla)*
- 1/2 cup water *(agua)*
- 1 large egg *(huevo)*
- 1 cup milk (whole or 2%) *(leche)*
- 1 teaspoon vanilla extract *(esencia de vainilla)*
- 1 1/2 cups finely shredded carrot *(zanahoria)*
- 1/2 cup raisins *(pasas)*
- cooking spray *(aceite en spray)*

Frosting:
- 220 grams (1 cup) cream cheese *(queso crema)*
- 1/3 cup powdered sugar *(azúcar en polvo)*
- 2 teaspoons fresh *mandarino* lime juice *(jugo de limón mandarino)*
- 1 tablespoon shredded coconut *(coco rallado)*

Directions:

1. Preheat oven to 350°F.

2. To prepare cake, lightly spoon flours into dry measuring cups; level with a knife. Combine flours, oats, cinnamon, baking powder, baking soda, and salt in a bowl and set aside.

3. Place brown sugar and butter in a large bowl; beat with a mixer at medium speed until well blended.

4. Add water and egg; beat well.

5. Beat in milk and vanilla.

6. Gradually add flour mixture, stirring just until blended.

7. Fold in carrot and raisins.

8. Spoon batter into a loaf pan coated with cooking spray. Bake at 350°F for 1 hour or until a wooden toothpick inserted in center comes out clean. Cool in pan 10 minutes on a wire rack; remove from pan. Cool completely on wire rack.

9. To prepare frosting, place cream cheese and powdered sugar in a bowl; beat with a mixer at medium speed until fluffy. Beat in lime juice & add coconut. Spread frosting over top of cooled cake.

Modifications I made to the original recipe:

- The original recipe called for 1/2 cup of soy flour which they don't carry in the grocery stores in my town. Instead, I increased the whole wheat and all-purpose flours by 1/4 cup each.
- I used 2% milk instead of whole milk, which the original recipe called for.
- The original recipe called for golden raisins, which I have not seen here in Costa Rica, so I used regular raisins.
- The cream cheese frosting originally called for lemon juice, however I haven't seen a yellow lemon at the market since we've been here. You could use lemon or lime juice, but I used the local orange-fleshed "*limón mandarino*," also called a "sour orange" by some.

- The original recipe called for a 4 oz block (1 cup) of cream cheese; locally it comes in 220 gram tubs.
- We like coconut, and its popular here, so I added some shredded coconut to the icing.

Bonus Recipes from Costa Rica Bloggers and Cooks

Jen Beck Seymour

Jen Beck Seymour, aka the "Costa Rica Chica," has written four books about Costa Rica, including *Costa Rica Chica: Retiring Early, Simplifying My Life, & Realizing that Less is Best*, and the *Costa Rica Chica Cookbook: Stirring Up My Favorite North American Recipes In Costa Rica*. Here are a couple of her delicious recipes.

Tomato Basil Soup

Warning - this soup is addicting. It honestly tastes like La Madeleine's, creamy and so flavorful. Fresh basil is best. MUST eat with my No-Knead Rustic Bread for dipping!

Servings: 12 mug size cups

Ingredients:

- 8-10 medium/large sized tomatoes – blanched*, peeled and cored (substitution = two 15 ounce cans of diced or whole tomatoes)
- 1 tablespoon minced garlic
- 1 small can of Maggi's Pasta de Tomate (USA substitution = 1 small can tomato paste)
- 4 cups water
- 14 large basil leaves, plus more for garnish (substitute: 2 1/2 to 3 tablespoons dried basil)

- ◆ 1 small box *crema dulce* stored at room temperature (USA substitution = 1 cup of refrigerated heavy whipping cream)
- ◆ 1/4 – 1/2 cup cream cheese (optional – this makes it even more creamy)
- ◆ 1 stick unsalted butter (I have used 1/2 stick before, still good)
- ◆ 2 teaspoons cracked black pepper
- ◆ 1 teaspoon salt (to taste)
- ◆ To serve: Parmesan cheese, basil leaves, pepper and No-Knead Rustic Bread

Directions:

1. Combine the tomatoes, garlic, Maggi's, water and basil leaves in a large saucepan.

2. Bring to a boil, then cover and simmer on low heat for 30 minutes.

3. After 30 minutes, add the *crema dulce*, cream cheese (if using), butter, pepper and salt. Cover and heat for 10 minutes.

4. Remove from heat, puree with a hand-held immersion blender. (If you do not have one, cool soup slightly and puree in batches in a blender.)

5. Garnish with grated Parmesan, basil leaves, and pepper and enjoy with a hot loaf of my No-Knead Rustic Bread.

Notes:

- ▪ This soup freezes well.
- ▪ Blanching tomatoes: Cut out top stems and cut a cross pattern on the bottoms of each tomato. Drop into a large pot of boiling water for 10-20 seconds, scoop out and put in ice bath for 10 seconds or so. Use a knife to peel the skin off – it will come off very easily.

Jen's No-Knead Rustic Bread

Who wants to knead bread all day? Not me! I love this recipe — it is easy and it truly makes the BEST bread. This is a beautiful artisan style loaf, which is crusty on the outside and soft and airy on the inside.

Servings: 4 small loaves

Ingredients:

- ♦ 6 1/4 cups flour
- ♦ 1 1/2 tablespoons salt
- ♦ 1 1/2 tablespoons yeast
- ♦ 3 cups warm water

Directions:

1. In a large re-sealable plastic container (mine is 6" high and 9" diameter) add flour with salt and yeast sprinkled on top. Add 3 cups warm water and stir with a wooden spoon until a loose, sticky dough forms. When there are no more pockets of unmixed flour or water left, put a towel over the top of the container, and let the dough sit at room temperature until it doubles in size (I live at an elevation of 4700 ft., so I let mine rise 6 hours).

2. When the dough has risen, fit the lid onto the container and seal it. Place the container in the fridge for a few hours, or overnight. This dough will keep in the fridge for 3 weeks. (I've also taken some dough at this point and baked it right away, but it is easier to work with if you refrigerate for at least a couple of hours.)

3. Preheat your oven for 30 minutes at 450° Fahrenheit (232° Celsius) with a covered Dutch oven* inside. Scoop out a hunk of the dough (grapefruit size). Turn dough in hands, gently stretching surface of dough, rotating ball a quarter-turn as you go, creating a rounded top and pinch bottom together. Set out on floured surface, sprinkle a bit of flour on top, and cover with towel for 30 minutes while the oven preheats.

COOKING IN COSTA RICA

4. When the oven is pre-heated, using a serrated knife, slash top of dough in three parallel, 1/4 inch deep cuts. Flour your hands and place dough in hot Dutch oven, cover, and bake for 30 minutes. Uncover and bake for 10-20 minutes more (time depends on your oven - you want it nice and crusty on top when done.)

5. NON-Dutch oven way: You can make a "*faux* Dutch oven" by using a metal pie plate and make a "tented" aluminum foil cover (you will need room for the dough to rise while it bakes). Bake with the instructions above (removing foil cover after 30 minutes). The secret of the Dutch oven (*faux* or real) is that it traps the moisture inside the loaf when it first begins to bake, giving it the air pockets and chewiness that is so delectable.

Alex Corral

Alex Corral is a Mexican chef living and cooking in Costa Rica. He also teaches at *Sabores La Escuela*, the first center for gastronomic studies in Costa Rica. While he enjoys a variety of international cuisines, his first love is to bring a taste of Mexico to much of his cooking. He is also the owner of the Chocolate Tour Costa Rica in La Garita, where you can learn about the origins of chocolate, how cacao is grown and processed, and how it has been traditionally used in cooking. You can even make your own chocolate candy during the tour.

Here are a couple of Chef Alex's signature recipes, using ingredients locally available in Costa Rica.

Pico de Gallo and Guacamole

Every good guacamole starts with a sauce called *"pico de gallo,"* also known as "Mexican sauce" since it has all the colors of the Mexican flag. Cilantro is indispensable to a good guacamole.

Pico de Gallo Ingredients:

- 450 grams onion
- 450 grams tomato
- 50 grams cilantro
- Lemon juice (enough to soak the whole mix of vegetables)
- Salt and pepper
- Cayenne pepper to taste

Directions:

1. Mince the onion as small as possible, put in a bowl and add salt. After a few minutes the onion will "sweat" (lose its juices by action of the salt). Drain that liquid.

2. Add lemon juice to cover the onion and let it rest.

3. Remove the seeds from the tomato and dice. Add to the onions.

4. Remove the leaves from the cilantro and chop them finely.

5. Season with the cayenne pepper.

Guacamole Ingredients:

- 2 or more avocados
- prepared *pico de gallo*

Note:

The most important ingredient in guacamole is the avocado. I recommend you use Hass avocados for this recipe. When you choose the avocados, look for a black shell. The flesh should be firm but allow a bit of pressure. You want them not too hard or too soft.

Directions:

1. Cut the avocados in half and carefully remove the pits with a knife. Scoop the avocado flesh from the shells and put into a bowl. Mash the avocados with a potato masher or other implement until you reach a creamy, uniform texture.

2. Little by little, add some of the *pico de gallo* to the mashed avocado. Make sure you use a slotted spoon so you can drain off some of the liquid before adding the Pico de Gallo to the avocado. The final mix and consistency depends on your personal taste. I like a very creamy guacamole with small touches of color from the vegetables. However, you want the avocado to be the dominant flavor.

3. Serve with tortilla chips or thin slices of carrot or cucumber.

Chef Alex's Roast Beef

Roast beef is an old British dish and is very tasty. In Costa Rica, the cut of meat used is called *mano de piedra*.

Ingredients:

- 1 kilo *mano de piedra de res* (eye of round)

For the Marinade:
- Sea salt to sprinkle around the meat, maybe 3 or 4 grams
- Worcestershire sauce - enough to soak the meat
- 4 or 5 bay leaves

Directions:

1. Make the marinade by combining the sea salt, Worcestershire sauce, and bay leaves. Pour the marinade over the beef and refrigerate for at least 12 hours.

2. After marinating, remove the beef and put on a baking sheet. Roast in the oven at 350 degrees in the oven for approximately 20 minutes per side, 40 minutes in total. The beef will be pink inside but not bloody.

3. Chill thoroughly. (A trick is to put it briefly in the freezer, just until it gets firm.) Slice very thin and use it in salads, sandwiches, or a cold meat platter.

COOKING IN COSTA RICA

Deby Hogue

Native Californian, Deby Hogue, retired to the jungle in Costa Rica with her surfer husband, Chuck. She loves to cook and bake and publishes her recipes on her blog, "Cooking in the Jungle." She learned to cook from her husband's Grandma, Marie, who was from Italy, and everything she makes has a bit of Grandma Marie in it. I especially love Deby's food photography, though it was difficult to choose a couple of recipes for this book since everything looked so good!

Grandma Marie's Pizza Dough

This is not thin crust. I know many people love thin crust nowadays and I do too, but sometimes I crave the thick, yeasty flavor and smell of this fluffy dough of Grandma Marie's.

This recipe makes 2 cookie sheet pizza's, so one is a pizza and one is a Focaccia with rosemary, garlic and sea salt. So good with a glass of wine.

Ingredients:

- 6 cups of flour
- 1 package of yeast (2 1/4 teaspoons)
- 1 tablespoon of salt
- 1 tablespoon of sugar
- 1 cup of lukewarm water
- 1/4 cup of oil (I use olive oil)
- 1 cup of hot milk

Directions:

1. Dissolve yeast in warm water, add to the hot milk.

2. In a mixing bowl, add salt, sugar and flour and combine.

3. Add liquids to the dry ingredients and knead well (8 to 10 minutes).

4. Put dough in a clean, large bowl and let rise 3 hours.

5. When risen, shape into pizzas. If it does not stretch at first, let it rest about 10 minutes and it will.

6. Add the sauce and whatever toppings you like and bake in a 400 degree oven for 20 to 30 minutes or until golden and the cheese is all melty.

Corn Fritters with Aioli Mayo and Cilantro Sauce

I love these corn fritters. You can add what you like; for me it's jalapeño, sometimes a little onion or cilantro. Any way you make them they are so good. I love them with an arugula salad. You can dip them in aioli mayo, cilantro sauce, or both.

4 Servings

Ingredients:

- 2 eggs, beaten
- 1/3 cup flour or a little more if you need it
- 2 tablespoons of grated Parmesan
- 2 garlic cloves mashed with a pinch of salt
- 1 jalapeño
- 2 cups of corn kernels
- pepper
- 3 tablespoons of oil for frying

Directions:

1. Put everything in the food processor and pulse until combined, but not too much, about 10 times.

2. Heat the oil in a fry pan and let it get good and hot. Put large tablespoons of batter carefully into hot oil. Fry about 3-4 minutes per side, drain on paper towels, sprinkle with salt, and try not to eat every last one, like me.

Aioli Mayo Ingredients:

- 1/2 cup of mayonnaise
- 2 cloves of garlic mashed with a pinch of salt
- 2 teaspoons of Dijon mustard
- 2 teaspoons of lemon juice
- 1 teaspoon of olive oil

Directions:

Combine all the ingredients in a small bowl and let stand in fridge for at least 1/2 hour.

Cilantro Sauce Ingredients:

- 1 bunch cilantro, cleaned
- pinch of salt
- 1 garlic clove
- squeeze of half a lemon or more
- 1 jalapeño
- 1 cup of yogurt or sour cream or half & half

Directions:

Put all ingredients in a food processor or blender, whip it all up, and enjoy on salad, fish tacos or with corn fritters.

Pat Wegner

Pat Wegner spent most of her 20s in Costa Rica, but it wasn't until 2011 that she returned with her husband, John, to live here permanently. Officially retired, they now live in Atenas, Costa Rica. Pat writes a blog called *"Mi Chunche"* (My Thingamajig) with a recipe section called *"Mi Chunche..en la cocina,"* which translates to "My Thingamajig...in the kitchen." Here are a couple of her favorite recipes.

Pineapple Salsa (Salsa Piña)

When we lived in Houston, Texas, one of our favorite places to dine was at an upscale Latino restaurant, called the Cafe Red Onion. They have an amazing menu of Latin fusion meals representing the best of Latin American cooking. Like most TexMex restaurants, they too serve chips and salsa when they take your beverage order, but their salsa is probably unlike any salsa you've encountered.

Since we have been here in Costa Rica for almost 4 years now, I was really craving some of Red Onion's salsa, so I began my internet search. I found the *Houston Chronicle* had actually published the recipe years ago from one of their readers. She got the recipe in a cooking class taught by Cafe Red Onion owner, Rafael Galindo.

The key ingredient calls for canned pineapple! Since we live here in the land of abundant fresh pineapple, canned pineapple would never be acceptable. So, I set about tweaking the recipe just a bit to take advantage of our fresh ingredients.

We served this salsa to dinner guests and received rave reviews. Enjoy!

Ingredients:

- 1 large fresh pineapple cut into chunks, with juice
- 1 tablespoon extra virgin olive oil
- 1/4 cup cilantro leaves, with the woody stems removed
- Juice of 1 juicy lime
- 1 fresh jalapeño pepper, seeded (more or less to taste)

- Salt to taste
- 1 packet of sugar substitute (optional)

Directions:

1. Combine 1/2 of the pineapple and all the other ingredients, except the salt and sugar substitute, in a blender or food processor. Pulse the blender until the cilantro and jalapeño are well chopped and mixed with the pineapple. Empty contents of blender into a bowl.

2. Add the remaining 1/2 of the pineapple to the blender and pulse just until you have small chunks/tidbits. Add this to the bowl with the other ingredients. Mix well.

3. Season to taste with salt, and with sugar substitute if the pineapple needs additional sweetness. Serve with chips.

¡Buen Provecho!

Vegetable Bouillon Paste

I found this idea on the internet, and I think it will quickly become a staple in my kitchen. This can be made with any of your favorite vegetables and is only limited by your imagination. The first time I made this, I only made a half batch and gave too much of it away to friends. Next time I will make the full 2 kilos so I don't run out of this so fast. So far, I have used it to make chicken & pasta soup, baked potato soup, and spaghetti sauce. I'm sure I'm going to find many more uses.

Ingredients:

- 250 grams leeks
- 125 grams broccoli
- 250 grams carrots
- 125 grams sweet peppers
- 125 grams onion
- 4 to 6 garlic cloves
- 125 grams parsley
- 125 grams cilantro
- 1 cup fine salt (I like to use our swimming pool salt because it is very fine and absolutely pure, no iodine, no fluoride, and no anti-caking ingredient.)

Directions:

1. Thoroughly wash all the vegetables and air dry as much as possible.
2. Coarse chop all the vegetables.
3. Smash garlic cloves and remove the peel.
4. Rough chop the herbs.
5. Process in a food processor until paste-like.
6. Weigh the processed ingredients and add the appropriate amount of salt.
   a. 2 kilos of ingredients (or 4.4 pounds): Add 1 cup of salt.

b. 1 kilo of ingredients (or 2.2 pounds): Add 1/2 cup of salt.

c. 1/2 kilo of ingredients (or 1.1 pounds): Add 1/4 cup of salt.

7. Freeze in small jars, but keep one in the fridge for quick meals. The basic recipe makes three to four 1/2 pint jars (but it halves well).

8. Use 1 teaspoon per cup of water in your recipes.

Notes:

- I know it sounds like too much salt, but you'll have to trust me on this. The salt is a natural preservative and you have to use a sufficient quantity to prevent the growth of bacteria. The great thing about using this vegetable bouillon in a recipe is that you will not need any additional salt.
- Think about adding basil, rosemary, oregano, spinach, kale, cauliflower, cabbage, sun-dried tomatoes, or anything else you like for some variation in the recipe. I'm sure you will come up with your favorite combination.
- Credit to www.food52.com for this idea.

John Michael Arthur

John Michael Arthur (*Juan Miguel* to his Tico friends) and his husband, Mike, retired to Costa Rica in 2014. They live on a beautiful 3.5 acre farm, complete with a river, in the Orosi Valley. John Michael spends his life now as what one of his heroes, Thomas Jefferson, called a "gentleman farmer." His days are spent tending to over 125 fruit trees in the orchard, milking the goats for homemade ice cream and cheeses, gathering eggs from the chickens, ducks, and geese, and finding creative ways to use the river and land.

I have personally tasted his ice creams and cheeses and they are spectacularly delicious! He has even started selling his cheeses in various Central Valley locations.

Vanilla Ice Cream Base & Variations

Ingredients:

- 2 cups heavy cream*
- 1 cup whole milk (I use goat's milk, of course)
- 1 cup sugar
- 2 tablespoons plain corn syrup
- 6 egg yolks
- 1/4 teaspoon salt
- 2 teaspoons vanilla

Directions:

1. Slowly heat milk, cream, and corn syrup to 145 degrees Fahrenheit over medium heat. Whip eggs yolks, sugar and salt together. Once milk is warm, temper the eggs with the milk mixture and then add back to the milk mixture. Over medium heat, raise temperature to 170 degrees Fahrenheit, stirring constantly.

2. Cool to tepid temperature and add vanilla. Cover and refrigerate overnight before freezing. Carefully remove cover and pour off the condensation (don't allow it to fall back into the cream). Freeze

according to your ice cream freezer's directions. Then ripen in the freezer for at least 6 hours.

3. Makes approximately 1 quart. Can be doubled or tripled.

*Note:

It's best to use the fresh *crema dulce* in the white bags with blue letters from Dos Pinos. It's just like our heavy whipping cream. Most gringos say it doesn't exist here, but I get it all the time at Walmart and sometimes at Auto Mercado. Also, any place (even *pulperias* that carry milk) can order it for you. You can use the shelf-stable *crema dulce* in the boxes - it produces acceptable results but tends to be a little "greasy" on your tongue.

Variations:

For quick and easy variations, you can stir in various Tico jams as soon as you remove the cream from the 170 degree heat. Reduce sugar to 3/4 cup and omit the corn syrup. Also, you can add other ingredients to make it as "gourmet" as you'd like. Some fruits benefit from adding 1 teaspoon almond extract instead of vanilla - you be the judge. Here are some examples:

Very Vanilla:

Increase vanilla to 1 tablespoon and stir in 1 tablespoon of peach jelly (it's the secret ingredient and no one will think it tastes like peach but it really boosts the vanilla.)

Berry and Black Pepper:

Add *mermelada de mora* (blackberry marmalade) to taste (about 1/2 C) and 1 teaspoon black pepper.

Strawberry Balsamic:

Add *mermelada de fresa* (strawberry marmalade) and balsamic vinegar to taste (about 2 teaspoons).

Salted Caramel:

Increase salt to be able to definitely taste it (I use about 3/4 teaspoon) and mix in Dulce de Leche from the squeeze bag to taste.

Coffee:

Infuse the 1 cup of milk with 1/3 cup ground coffee. Steep until very strong. Strain grounds through sieve (don't worry that some very small bits of grounds escape - it's good).

Coffee Toffee:

Make as for coffee ice cream and then add your favorite toffee in small chunks just before placing ice cream in the regular freezer to ripen.

Chocolate Ice Cream Base & Variations

Ingredients:

- 2 cups of heavy cream*
- 1 cup of milk
- 1 cup of sugar
- 1/3 cup unsweetened cocoa powder
- 2 teaspoons vanilla
- 5 egg yolks
- 1/4 teaspoon salt

Directions:

1. Mix cocoa and half the sugar in saucepan and stir to thoroughly incorporate the cocoa into the sugar. Then, add just enough cream to make a thick slurry. Heat slowly and stir constantly to blend well and remove any lumps.

2. When smooth, slowly add the rest of the cream and the milk and heat to 145 degrees Fahrenheit.

3. Whip together eggs and remaining sugar and salt. Temper eggs with heated milk. Return to pan and heat to 170 degrees Fahrenheit.

4. Cool as for vanilla base above. Freeze as above.

*Note:

It's best to use the fresh *crema dulce* in the white bags with blue letters from Dos Pinos. It's just like our heavy whipping cream. Most gringos say it doesn't exist here, but I get it all the time at Walmart and sometimes at Auto Mercado. Also, any place (even *pulperias* that carry milk) can order it for you. You can use the shelf-stable *crema dulce* in the boxes - it produces acceptable results but tends to be a little "greasy" on your tongue.

Variations:

Rocky Road (*Calle Pedregosa*):

Add slivered almonds and small marshmallows

Chocolate Fire:

Add 1/8 to 1/4 teaspoon cayenne pepper according to your taste, for amazing flavor and only a mild burn at the end of the sweet chocolate flavor.

U.S. Measure to Metric Conversion Guide

Temperature

Temperature Conversion Chart

(Rounded to the nearest degree Celsius)

Fahrenheit	Celsius
100°F	38°C
150°F	66°C
200°F	93°C
250°F	121°C
275°F	135°C
300°F	149°C
325°F	163°C
350°F	177°C
375°F	191°C
400°F	204°C
425°F	218°C
450°F	232°C
475°F	246°C
500°F	260°C
550°F	288°C
600°F	316°C

Volume

Volume Conversion Chart for liquids, herbs, spices, baking powder, yeast, *etc.*

(Rounded to the nearest ounce or milliliter)

U.S. Fluid Measures		Metric
1/8 teaspoon		.625 ml.
1/5 teaspoon		1 ml.
1/4 teaspoon		1.25 ml.
1/2 teaspoon		2.5 ml.
3/4 teaspoon		3.75 ml.
1 teaspoon		5 ml.
1 tablespoon	.5 fluid oz.	15 ml.
1 1/2 tablespoons	.8 fluid oz.	22.5 ml.
1/8 cup	1 fluid oz.	30 ml.
1/5 cup	1.7 fluid ozs.	50 ml.
1/4 cup	2 fluid ozs.	59 ml.
1/3 cup	2.7 fluid ozs.	80 ml.
2/5 cup	3.4 fluid ozs.	100 ml.
1/2 cup	4 fluid ozs.	118 ml.
2/3 cup	5.3 fluid ozs.	158 ml.
3/4 cup	6 fluid ozs.	177 ml.
1 cup	8 fluid ozs.	237 ml.
1 1/2 cups	12 fluid ozs.	355 ml.
2 cups (1 pint)	16 fluid ozs.	473 ml.
3 cups (1 1/2 pints)	24 fluid ozs.	710 ml.
4 cups (2 pints / 1 quart)	32 fluid ozs.	946 ml.
4.2 cups (1.06 qts. / .26 gal.)	34 fluid ozs.	1 liter
4 quarts (1 gal.)	128 fluid ozs.	3.8 liters

Cooking Measurement Equivalents:

3 teaspoons = 1 tablespoon
1 tablespoon = 1/16 cup
2 tablespoons = 1/8 cup
2 tablespoons + 2 teaspoons = 1/6 cup
4 tablespoons = 1/4 cup
5 tablespoons + 1 teaspoon = 1/3 cup
6 tablespoons = 3/8 cup
8 tablespoons = 1/2 cup
10 tablespoons + 2 teaspoons = 2/3 cup
12 tablespoons = 3/4 cup
16 tablespoons = 1 cup
48 teaspoons = 1 cup
2 cups = 1 pint
2 pints = 1 quart

Abbreviations:

teaspoon = t.
Tablespoon = T.
cup = C.
ounce/ounces - oz./ozs.
pint/pints = pt./pts.
quart/quarts = qt./qts.
gallon = gal.
milliliters = ml.
liters = L.

Special Notes:

1 packet of dry yeast = 2 1/4 teaspoons = 11.25 ml.
1/2 cup butter = 1 stick = 4 ounces = 115 grams
1 cup butter = 2 sticks = 8 ounces = 230 grams

Weight

Weight Conversion Chart

(Rounded to the nearest gram or ounce)

Imperial	Metric
.035 ounce	1 gram
1 ounce	28 grams
1/8 pound / 2 ozs.	57 grams
3.5 ozs.	100 grams
1/4 pound / 4 ozs.	113 grams
1/3 pound / 5.3 ozs.	150 grams
6 ozs.	170 grams
1/2 pound / 8 ozs.	227 grams
2/3 pound / 10.6 ozs.	300 grams
3/4 pound / 12 ozs.	340 grams
1 pound / 16 ozs.	454 grams
1.1 pounds	1/2 kg. / 500 grams
2 pounds / 32 ozs.	907 grams
2.205 pounds / 35 ozs.	1 kg. / 1000 grams

Estimated Weight Conversions of Basic Ingredients:

1/4 cup flour = 35 grams
1/2 cup flour = 70 grams
3/4 cup flour = 105 grams
1 cup flour = 140 grams
1/4 cup sugar = 50 grams
1/3 cup sugar = 70 grams
1/2 cup sugar = 100 grams
2/3 cup sugar = 135 grams
3/4 cup sugar = 150 grams
1 cup sugar = 200 grams
1/4 cup powdered sugar = 40 grams
1/2 cup powdered sugar = 80 grams
3/4 cup powdered sugar = 120 grams
1 cup powdered sugar = 160 grams
1/2 cup butter = 1 stick = 4 ounces = 115 grams
1 cup butter = 2 sticks = 8 ounces = 230 grams
1 tablespoon heavy cream = 15 grams
1/4 cup heavy cream = 60 grams
1/2 cup heavy cream = 115 grams
3/4 cup heavy cream = 175 grams
1 cup heavy cream = 230 grams

Abbreviations:

grams = g.
kilograms = kg.
pound = lb.
pounds = lbs.
ounce = oz.
ounces = ozs.

Length

Length Conversion Chart

(Metric equivalents are rounded up to the nearest .1 millimeter or centimeter)

Inches	Metric Equivalent	
1/8 inch	3.2 mm.	.32 cm.
1/4 inch	6.4 mm.	.64 cm.
1/2 inch	12.7 mm.	1.3 cm.
3/4 inch	19 mm.	1.9 cm.
1 inch	25.4 mm.	2.5 cm.
2 inches	50.8 mm.	5.1 cm.
3 inches	76.2 mm.	7.6 cm.
4 inches	101.6 mm.	10.2 cm.
5 inches	127 mm.	12.7 cm.
6 inches	152.4 mm.	15.2 cm.
7 inches	177.8 mm.	17.8 cm.
8 inches	203.2 mm.	20.3 cm.
9 inches	228.6 mm.	22.9 cm.
10 inches	254 mm.	25.4 cm.
11 inches	279.4 mm.	27.9 cm.
1 foot / 12 inches	304.8 mm.	30.5 cm.

Abbreviations:

inch = in.
millimeter = mm.
centimeter = cm.

Resources

Retire for Less in Costa Rica Resources

Retire for Less in Costa Rica
http://retireforlessincostarica.com/

My husband, Paul, and I started our website in 2008. It is a trusted source of practical information for folks considering a move to Costa Rica as well as for those who have already made their homes here. Every month, we publish our detailed cost of living report, plus an annual summary. We also write about topics of interest such as healthcare (both private and the public *Caja* system), crime, daily life, culture, gardening, and living a more simple life.

You can read about why we chose to live in San Ramón in these articles:

- *The 10 Reasons Why We Chose San Ramón de Alajuela*
  http://retireforlessincostarica.com/10-reasons-we-chose-san-ramon-de-alajuela/
- *The 7 Reasons Why We Still Choose San Ramón*
  http://retireforlessincostarica.com/the-7-reasons-why-we-still-choose-san-ramon/

And here is a small sampling of other popular articles available on our website:

- *Reinventing Yourself in Retirement*
  http://retireforlessincostarica.com/reinventing-yourself-in-retirement/

- *Our 2016 Annual Cost of Living in Costa Rica Summary*
  http://retireforlessincostarica.com/our-2016-annual-cost-of-living-in-costa-rica-summary/
- *9 Tips to Find Your "Perfect Place" in Costa Rica*
  http://retireforlessincostarica.com/9-tips-to-find-your-perfect-place-in-costa-rica/
- *Costa Rica's Caja: How it Works*
  http://retireforlessincostarica.com/costa-ricas-caja-how-it-works/

We invite you to sign up for our free newsletter by using the form on any page of our website. When you subscribe, you will receive our special report, "The Top 10 Qualities of a Successful Expat in Costa Rica," as a thank-you gift.

Retire for Less in Costa Rica Relocation Tours

The goal of all our tours is to save you time and money, while showing you the possibilities. We do this in three ways:

- by having you meet and speak with other expats in your selected towns, when possible,
- by giving you a real sense of what it's like to live in that town, and
- by customizing the experience to answer your specific questions.

We specialize in the western Central Valley, most often San Ramón, Grecia, and Atenas, as well as Lake Arenal. We have also taken folks to places like Zarcero, Orosi, Playa Esterillos Este, Heredia, Escazú, Santa Ana, Puriscal, and San Jose.

We can customize the tour to see anything you like, but we usually look at medical care options, a pharmacy, a health food store, a grocery store, the feria (local farmers' market), cultural activities, a walking tour of the center of town, a driving tour of some of the neighborhoods, and anything else you would like to do.

For pricing and more information, please contact us at:

> Paul & Gloria Yeatman
> Email: info@retireforlessincostarica.com
> 8919-2710 in Costa Rica
> 410-665-4961 from the U.S.
> +011-506-8919-2710 Internationally
> +506-8919-2710 WhatsApp

We would be happy to help you decide whether, or not, Costa Rica is right for you.

Retire for Less in Costa Rica Ultimate Healthcare Tour
http://retireforlessincostarica.com/our-ultimate-healthcare-tour-of-costa-rica/

Our Ultimate Healthcare Tour is the only tour designed to demystify Costa Rica's healthcare system. Our blend of personal insights and on-the-ground experience combines to answer your questions about whether or not Costa Rica's healthcare system could meet your individual needs. We cover both Costa Rica's public system (known as the "*Caja*") as well as private options for both healthcare and insurance. While it focuses on healthcare, you will also learn about living and retiring in Costa Rica's Central Valley. To find out more about our Ultimate Healthcare Tour and to see a sample itinerary, please visit the webpage above.

Cooking in Costa Rica

Cooking in Costa Rica Facebook group
https://www.facebook.com/groups/764298813625584/

Cooking in Costa Rica is a group dedicated to helping expats cook delicious meals using local and easily accessible ingredients.

Deby Hogue's cooking blog, "Cooking in the Jungle"
https://www.cookinginthejungle.com/

Pat Wegner's cooking blog, *"Mi Chunchi...en la Cocina"*
http://enlacocina.michunche.com

Food-Related Attractions

Alex Corral's Chocolate Tour Costa Rica
http://www.choco-tour.com/

> The Chocolate Tour provides a close encounter with cacao and its 4,500 years of history. You can even make your own chocolate! While you are there, be sure to visit the medical herbs and super foods garden.

Finca Luna Nueva Tours
http://fincalunanuevalodge.com/tour/farm-tour/
http://fincalunanuevalodge.com/tour/sacred-seeds-tour/

> *Finca Luna Nueva's* Farm Tour is probably unlike any other farm you've ever visited or even imagined. Here, they grow the healthiest food to serve to farm guests in their restaurant. Their food production goes "beyond organic," regenerating both topsoil and biological diversity.

> The Sacred Seeds Sanctuary at *Finca Luna Nueva* currently houses over 300 tropical medicinal plants. It is a dynamic collection that both protects and celebrates the biological diversity in Costa Rica and the tropics.

Espíritu Santo Coffee Tour
http://espiritusantocoffeetour.com/tour/?lang=en

> Learn how coffee is grown, processed, and brewed in the traditional Costa Rican way while touring this working coffee plantation.

Grocery Shopping

Auto Mercado
http://www.automercado.cr/localidades-y-horarios/

Locate the closest *Auto Mercado* to you at the webpage above.

PriceSmart
https://shop.pricesmart.com/cr/en/about/club-locations

Locate the closest PriceSmart location to you at the webpage above.

Cúrcuma
https://www.curcumacr.com/

Located in Escazú, *Cúrcuma* carries a wide range of natural and international products. They specialize in herbs and spices, seeds, teas, nutritional supplements, essential oils, and much more. It is a good place to locate those hard-to-find spices and seasonings.

Hacienda Sur Artisan Beef
http://haciendasur.com/butcher-shop/

Hacienda Sur doesn't "produce beef." Instead, they "raise cattle" in a pristine, natural environment, free of hormones, antibiotics, herbicides, pesticides, and stress.

Shopping Organic

Upward Spirals
http://upwardspirals.net

The Upward Spirals Organic Directory includes a list of organic producers and suppliers in Costa Rica, organizations supporting organic farmers, and free resources on organic farming and permaculture. It was updated in July 2017. The Organic Directory is available for free download in both English and Spanish at the following webpages:
- Download the Organic Directory in English at: https://upwardspirals.net/organic-directory/
- Download the Organic Directory in Spanish at: http://upwardspirals.net/directorio-organico/

Feria Verde farmers' market
https://www.facebook.com/FeriaVerde/

Feria Verde is located in Aranjuez, San Jose

Finca Organica Guadalupe
https://www.facebook.com/people/Finca-Organica-Guadalupe/100005480744893

Finca Organica Guadalupe is a certified organic farm located in Zarcero, Costa Rica

Finca Organica Tierra de Sueños
https://www.facebook.com/fincaorganicats/

Finca Organica Tierra de Sueños, located in Zarcero, is no longer certified organic; however, they still maintain their organic practices and values.

Other Food-Related Websites

Tropical Grazing Institute
http://tropicalgrazinginstitute.org/

> Their mission is to develop and improve sustainable practices for livestock production in tropical regions and to teach small farmers how to produce healthier meat, to better protect the environment, and in the process, to improve their economic opportunities.

Insight Guides: "The delicious fruit of Costa Rica: know your *anona* from your *zapote*"
https://www.insightguides.com/inspire-me/blog/costa-rican-fruit

Books for Further Reading

Costa Rica Chica Cookbook: Stirring Up My Favorite North American Recipes In Costa Rica
by Jen Beck Seymour

Eating Clean in Costa Rica: Simple, Easy Recipes from the Kitchen of Blue Osa and Chef Marie
by Chef Marie

Costa Rica Tropical Fruits Identification Guide
(Laminated Foldout Pocket Field Guide, English and Spanish Edition)
by Rainforest Publications

Frutas Tropicales de Costa Rica - Tropical Fruits of Costa Rica
(English and Spanish Text)
by Marcia Baraona Ellen Sancho

Recipe Index

About the Author

In her life before moving to Costa Rica, Gloria worked as a certified meeting and event planner, training and conference director, and business administrator. She left the 9-5 behind when she was 52 years old to embrace *Pura Vida* (the pure life) with her husband, Paul. The goal: to retire much earlier and less expensively than they could ever do in the U.S. They moved to Costa Rica on April 1, 2009 with 12 suitcases, one trunk, and one cat.

They developed retireforlessincostarica.com to give people who share their dream a place to learn about life in Costa Rica and how they, too, can "retire for less."

Paul and Gloria offer tours of the western Central Valley, Lake Arenal, and a comprehensive tour of healthcare in Costa Rica. They have been regular speakers at International Living's Fast Track Costa Rica Conferences and participated in nine other International Living Conferences throughout the U.S. and Mexico.

Gloria lives in San Ramón de Alajuela, with Paul and their two cats, Torí and Laura Chinchilla (named for the first female president of Costa Rica).

Gloria loves to cook, read recipes, and watch cooking shows. She also spends her time reading novels and books on health and nutrition, learning Spanish, volunteering, and speaking and writing about her favorite topic, life in Costa Rica.

Made in the USA
Middletown, DE
08 May 2023

30219671R00129